One of the Lucky Ones

Nicole Holland

One of the Lucky Ones

An Authorized Biography of Nicole Holland

By Brenda Hancock

May you be inspired.
Brenda Hancock

HANNOVER HOUSE
2013

ISBN 978-0-9837318-0-1   /   UPC 7-61450-87622-4

Published by Hannover House
1428 Chester St., Springdale, AR 72764
www.HannoverHouse.com

Text Editor: Debbie Upton
Text Designer: John Coghlan
Cover Art Design: Lindsay VanBeck

Printed in the United States of America

Library of Congress Cataloging-in-Publication Data

Hancock, Brenda, 1949-
One of the lucky ones : an authorized biography of Nicole Holland / by Brenda Hancock.
pages cm
ISBN 978-0-9837318-0-1 (tradeback)
1. Holland, Nicole. 2. World War, 1939-1945—Underground movements—France—Biography. 3. World War, 1939-1945—Personal narratives, French. 4. France—History—German occupation, 1940-1945—Biography. 5. Jews—France—Biography. I. Title.
D802.F8H36 2013
940.53'44092—dc23
[B]
                                                        2012044146

To my mother, Nicole, who lived such an incredible life and passed along a legacy of strength and courage; to my sister, Barbara, who urged me to write Mom's story; and to my husband, Don, who has patiently supported and encouraged me. My thanks and love to you all.

Contents

Preface

Having listened to my mother's stories as a child, I was always enthralled by her tales of World War II. Often my sister and I would become so wrapped up in her exciting adventures that we would have to hurriedly jump up from the breakfast table to get ready for school, worried that we might be late. In the early 1980s I first made an attempt at writing her story based on some notes my father had typed and my memories of her stories. When Mom read the first few pages, she said, "Well, it's a fine story, but it's not mine." As a result, I merely set it aside, not thinking of trying to get it right. About a year later, I did manage to write a poem that told her story in a compact manner, which I gave to her on Valentine's Day in 1984. Much to my surprise, she was thrilled with the poem. After Mom had celebrated her eightieth birthday, my sister urged me to try again, insisting that "we" get Mom's story down for our children before it was too late.

At first I wrote secretly, not even telling Mom what I was attempting, but it soon became apparent that I needed details to get it right. Telling her that Barbara had convinced me to record her story for our children and their children and all the children to come, I explained to Mom that I was trying again and that this time I wanted her to approve everything I was writing as I wrote. Anything she didn't agree with I would willingly change. I explained that I needed specific names, dates, and places and took notes as she filled in details for me. After completing a chapter, I would take it to her to read and approve or ask what changes she wanted me to make. Eventually, I managed to record her story in a way that she felt was truly "her story." From the beginning, the purpose of recording her story was to preserve it for her descendants. I wanted her grandchildren and great-grandchildren to be able to experience what my sister and I had throughout our youth, to feel as they read that they were sitting at the breakfast table learning about this incredible woman from whom they were descended. Because of this, I wrote the entire biography in first person, feeling it would more closely recreate for them the feeling of being there with her. May her story entrance you as it did my sister and me so many years ago and inspire you to bravely conquer whatever life brings to you.

CHAPTER 1

A Rich Beginning

One of the lucky ones—I guess that's how most people would think of me, and for the most part, they're probably right. I never understood why I ended up being one of the lucky ones. There were many who were much smarter than I could ever be, much more talented, more beautiful who weren't so lucky. I often wondered what it was about me that made me one of the lucky ones—still haven't figured that one out—guess I never will.

For the first eighteen years of my life, I knew I was one of the lucky ones simply because of the wonderful life that I had experienced. No, I wasn't from a wealthy family. I didn't have all the material possessions I wanted, along with all the privileges of the rich and famous. What I did have was worth much more than that. I grew up in a small apartment on what the French call the second floor but Americans refer to as the third floor at 10 Rue des Deux Ponts in the fourth arrondisement of Paris, France. Memories of that building, that apartment bring me nothing but joy. Specifically built in 1926 by Madame Fernand Halphen in memory of her husband, the building was designed for Jewish families who had many children. In designing the building, Madame Halphen kept in mind that there would be many children living there who would need a place to gather after school to allow their parents (most of whom worked at home) to have a few more hours of peace and quiet in which to do their work. To accommodate this situation, the building's ground floor was not taken up by apartments, but had a special area just for the children. Not only did Madame Halphen create the special area for the children to study and play after school, but she also hired two young ladies from social services to oversee the children while their parents worked. As a result, it wasn't like I just had the two sisters and one brother who lived with me, but almost a hundred brothers and sisters. We children in this building felt a special closeness that the children in other apartment buildings in our area didn't have.

During the school year we attended school several blocks away

Our apartment building.

BRENDA HANCOCK

at L'Ecole Rue des Hospitaliers St. Gervais, girls in one part of the school and boys in a separate part divided by a common kitchen. Although it was about a fifteen-minute walk to school from our building, we would all walk together and find ways to make the walk fun and not seem so long. We considered ourselves the lucky ones once again when we found out that because our teachers were Catholics or Protestants and most of us at the school were Jewish, we got both Jewish and Christian holidays. Who wouldn't feel lucky as a child to have extra holidays? From the age of three, all the children in the building would walk to the school, strictly follow the orders of our teachers for the length of the school day, and then walk home together. Once back in the apartment building, we would gather in the children's area to do our homework. Homework always had to be completed first before anything else. Lili and Lou, the two young ladies from social services, would make sure of that. Then when Lili moved on and went to Palestine, Mathia took her place, followed still later by Yette. These four young ladies made a great impact on all of us and were almost like older sisters as far as our affection for them was concerned. When Lili and Lou were sure we had met our obligations, we could have fun. They helped us make up and sing songs, put on plays, and do artwork, and they encouraged us to be creative in many ways. At dinner time we all went to our respective apartments for the evening meal with our parents and preparations for bed.

Our apartment was small by today's standards, but being kids, we thought it was very big and roomy. Upon opening the door, a visitor would be looking down what we thought of as a very long hallway. Beside the entry door was the WC or half bath as people call it today. The rest of the apartment consisted of two rooms to the left of the hallway and two to the right. In the first room on the left I slept with my sisters. My older sister Aimée was there until she got married, but Hélène, Madeleine, and I were

My parents, Berthe and Maurice Widerman.

always sharing that room. The next room on the left was my parents' bedroom. In there along with my parents' furniture was a roll-away bed with a lovely cover to hide it while it was folded up and not in use. This bed was for my younger brother Robert, who would sleep in the dining room or in winter in the kitchen so he could be warmer. Across from my parents' room was the kitchen. Here were the three sewing machines that my father used in his work as a tailor, along with a very long table, a big stove, and a cabinet with a sink and a burner. The sewing machines were lined up under the window for the extra light. Sometimes my mother would help my father at the machines, and when we were older, my sisters and I would take our turns at the extra sewing machines. Although I had two older brothers and six older sisters who were married with children of their own, my closest siblings were my older sister Hélène, my younger sister, Madeleine, and my baby brother, Robert. Although both my sisters Ida and Aimée had lived there with us before they married, I only remember when Aimée also lived there. For as long as I could remember, Ida was already married. So, there we were—six and sometimes seven people living and working in four rooms. Many might think of this as less than lucky, but they would be ignoring the love and security that filled that apartment.

For the most part, that love and security I felt growing up came from my mother. To each of her children, she was an angel. Somehow she managed to make each one of us feel as if we were her favorite child. Twenty years younger than my father, my mother married my father after his first wife had died and left him with the care of their five children. My half-sisters were Sarah, Fanny, Adèle, and Régine, and my half-brother was Henri. All of them had been born in Warsaw, Poland, and when my parents decided to migrate to France, Sarah and Régine stayed behind in Warsaw with their husbands and children. No one could consider my mother's life easy, first mothering her five stepchildren and then caring for the eight more she gave birth to herself. The children born to my mother and my father were Jacques (who was only three or four years younger than Henri), Ida, Aimée, Bernard, Hélène, me, Madeleine, and then Robert. My brother Bernard died when he was only two years old, which was before I was born. The story I always heard was that something was wrong with my sister Aimée, and she couldn't walk until she was four years old. Then once she walked, Bernard died suddenly. As far as I can remember, Bernard had not been ill before, and it seemed that the family thought Bernard had given his life so that Aimée would not be an invalid.

Any time any of these children or their children became sick, Mother was there to help nurse them back to health. Often my sisters and I had to give up our room for some relative who was sick and needed my mother, who willingly nursed them all back to health. Any other family members who came to visit would also come to our apartment, moving my sisters and me out to the floor of some other part of the apartment once again. Being one of the five younger ones, I ended up with nieces and nephews who were my age or even older. I always remember my mother as being a wonderful cook who looked like she enjoyed her own cooking very much. Most of her children inherited her wide nose and light blue eyes, and I can't remember her before her dark brown hair was sprinkled with gray. Despite our life of near poverty, I don't remember my mother ever complaining about her workload or responsibilities. I certainly thought she ought to from time to time. One thing in particular irks me to this day. I can remember my parents going to visit my father's older children on Saturdays. At least one of these children who had been raised by my mother after theirs had died would make my mother sit without even being offered a glass of water while they regaled their father with the best drinks and snacks they could get. Once Hélène and I were old enough to notice how they treated her, we were so angered that we refused to accompany them, and Hélène suggested she do the same. My mother would not hear of it. It was her duty to accompany her husband. She never complained, never refused to accompany my father on these visits to his children, and always treated these ingrates with respect and love. For this as well as everything else she did for us, her own children, my mother was the angel who made life so wonderful, made us all feel so very lucky.

Unlike my mother, my father was a rather slender, very reserved man who was very set in his ways. Perhaps he was so distant, so meticulous, and insistent on having things his way because he was already an "old" man by the time we four younger ones came along. Always well groomed, my father was a handsome man with a long, slender nose and a neatly trimmed goatee. I don't know if it was because he worked making clothing for people to make them look nice or just a quirk of his personality, but I never saw my father that he wasn't meticulously groomed and looking his best. The only one of his children that he favored was my younger brother Robert. When Robert would steal my father's special candy that none of us were supposed to touch, we were all sure Father knew who had done it, yet Robert was never punished. My parents had a "martinet" hanging on the wall to remind us to tow the line to avoid their using it on us. This instrument of punishment was made of a wooden handle from which was suspended numerous slender leather straps. Spankings with the "martinet" were something we all tried to avoid. Robert would sneak over to the "martinet" with a sharp pair of scissors and snip off the straps one at a time. None of us were unhappy with his efforts to reduce the punishment, and my father never said anything about it, even though it eventually became obvious what was happening.

My father loved the opera and would go periodically to enjoy this favorite pastime. Whenever he went, he would take Robert with him. Never did he invite any of us girls to go along, but Robert was always his companion on these outings. It may sound like we resented Robert for this special treatment, but he was such a darling little boy that we held no resentment at all. Our not being invited just served to increase the distance between us and our father since we had no common ground with this stern, quiet man. As much as he loved music, my father hated noise in the house, especially at the dinner table. He thought children were meant to be seen and not heard. His insistence on silence, especially at the dinner table, was a real problem for us. Naturally, we had a hard time containing our energy, and as hard as we tried, we would often burst into giggles when we were supposed to be quiet, much to the dissatisfaction of our father. This more than anything makes me remember him as a stern man, very unlike my gentle, loving mother.

Passport photo for the move from Poland to Paris. *Left to right:* sisters Ida, Hélène, Aimée, Berthe (mother), and me (the baby in my mother's lap).

Technically, only Madeleine and Robert were actually French, having been born after my parents moved to Paris. My parents had migrated from Warsaw in 1923 when I was about six months old. Hélène was just about a year older than I, and Mother ended up bringing us children to join my father, who had ventured to Paris with his brother a while before sending for the rest of us. Three of his older married children eventually made the move as well. Only my oldest half-sister, Sarah, and my youngest half-sister, Régine, remained in Warsaw with their husbands and children. I do remember Sarah coming for a visit in 1927 since I went to meet her and bring her home. My memory of her is of a very elegant, beautiful lady wearing a fur coat. For that visit, she came alone, so I never met her children. Régine and her younger daughter Adela came for a visit in 1936. I can remember that Régine wasn't as elegant nor as beautiful as Sarah—maybe it was the fur coat Sarah wore that gives me that impression because I have seen photos that show Régine was an attractive woman as well. My sisters and I tormented poor Adela, who only understood Polish and could not communicate with us. She and her mother never came back for another visit. Surely, it wasn't because we were so mean.

At home, my parents spoke Yiddish, not Polish, so that was my native language until I went to school at age three and learned to speak French. My mother also spoke French as well, probably due to her having to deal with merchants. Although I am almost certain he understood what we were saying, especially in our teenage years, my father never spoke French. I can remember some men from Russia coming for a visit and hearing my father speaking with them in Russian, but I never heard him utter a word of French despite our living there together for almost twenty years.

Madame Halphen, the generous lady who had built our apartment, was also responsible for the children of the building getting to vacation in the summertime on the coast of Normandy. Accompanied by Lili and Lou (and later Mathia and finally Yette,

Summer at Colleville: Sister Hélène, *second from right, standing on bottom row;* Sister Madeleine, *blonde on third row, fourth from right;* me, *fifth from right on top row.*

who came from a wealthy family), the boys would go one month to Colleville sur Mer (later known as Omaha Beach), and then we girls would go the next. Except for one terrible memory of a teenage boy saying he would teach me to swim and then holding my head under water until I was afraid I would drown, my memories of those summers at the coast just add to that feeling of being lucky. Our going gave our parents a break from us. At the same time, it gave us a chance to get fresh air and exercise while enjoying the sand, the sea, and the friendships. Although I never learned to swim and am still afraid to be in water that is deeper than my shoulders, I treasure those summers at Colleville.

At school, Madeleine was the smartest of the three of us. Not only was she blonde, blue-eyed, and pretty, but she also excelled at all the teachers asked her to do. Hélène had black wavy hair with green eyes, which made her a beauty in my mind as well as many others, but she was too head-strong and independent to care about whether she was the best in class or for that matter what anyone thought of her. In fact, at one point she decided to demote herself by several years so she could go back to the class of a teacher she liked rather than stay with a teacher she didn't like. As for me, I always considered myself as just average—not pretty like my sisters, eyes that were sometimes blue, sometimes gray, sometimes green, hair that was light brown and wildly curly, a body that was a little too heavy, and a brain that was not smart—I was just average. I did what was asked of me at school, but never received the accolades that Madeleine got. Unlike Hélène, I didn't even have a strong character to distinguish myself. However, I did have lots of friends, can remember people always referring to me as the "sweet" one, and feel certain that I was a welcome addition to our group of friends in the building.

Our darling little brother Robert seemed to have inherited all the talent in our family and several other families as well. Not only was he singing and dancing from the time he was about two years old, but he also excelled at art school. If it involved creativity, Robert mastered it. Even at the age of twelve, he was bringing in extra money from the entertainment gigs he and some of the boys from our building managed to get. Some of the extra money went to pay for lessons at the art school that my father insisted Robert attend. He never ceased to amaze and entertain us.

After finishing public school, Hélène began to study acting while working, first with my father at the sewing machines, and then outside the home. We heard from her teachers after she was taken to the concentration camps that if she had lived, she would have been the greatest actress in all of France, so maybe Robert hadn't inherited ALL of the family talent after all. As for me, I worked at the sewing machines with my father, too, for a while before finding work outside the home like Hélène had done.

Unlike Hélène and Robert, I had no special talents that needed nurturing. I expected that I would find a nice Jewish boy, marry him, and raise some children, trying to be as much like my own mother as possible. There was one boy in particular who lived in our building, David Zylberberg, who used to always go to the movies with me and a couple of friends. Thinking back on David, I realized he was my first love, and I could easily picture being married to him. However, those plans were only the dream of a distant future and one that never materialized due to World War II and the total upheaval of that wonderful life I had enjoyed, but not nearly appreciated enough. From our apartment house, David was one of the first to be taken, and not being one of the lucky ones like me, he never returned.

CHAPTER 2

The Nightmare Begins

Things first began to change on September 3, 1939—that's when France declared war on Germany. Of course, everyone had heard rumors and rumblings about what was going on to the east of France, but we really didn't think it would ever have anything to do with us. As older teenagers, Hélène and I would enjoy going to the movies and swooning over our favorite movie stars, Jean Servais, Clark Gable, Gary Cooper, and Errol Flynn, among others. Sometimes we would go skating or dancing, again accompanied by many of our friends from the building. Although money wasn't flowing freely, we always managed to have enough to enjoy these fun pastimes with our friends. I can remember once having gone skating earlier in the day and wanting to go to the movies later. My sisters and I had made up a language, thinking we could speak without our mother understanding. When I said to my sisters in that language that I wanted to go to the movies, my mother said, "I'm going to give you the movies!" There just wasn't enough money to do both activities in the same day, but more importantly it was surprising how smart our mother was—this lady who had not had much formal education had quickly deciphered our "code."

The rumors of war brought fear to many, including my parents. That summer of 1939, Robert had been in Cabourg, a coastal town on the English Channel near Caen in Lower Normandy, where his mentor, Madame Aron, had gotten him a job performing. Madeleine, Hélène, and I were not too far away in Colleville for our usual summer visit. Even though we were in our late teens, we were still invited to accompany the girls of the building for the month at Colleville. My parents became so worried that they left Paris to join Robert in Cabourg. A week after war was declared, they insisted that Madeleine, Hélène, and I join them in Cabourg as well. We all lived in a small apartment, waiting (impatiently for us kids) to see what would happen next. When school began again, Robert and Madeleine would go to school during the day, but Hélène and I had nothing to do except wait around. There were no jobs to be found. Madeleine helped the owners of the apartment after school, so life for her was fairly full. Hélène and I would walk the beaches, wondering how long we would have to remain there with nothing to do. I distinctly remember one day as we walked along, hearing the drone of airplane engines in the distance. We looked out to sea in time to witness one plane shoot another out of the sky. Incredulously, we saw the battered airplane dive into the English Channel and looked at each other in amazement at how our lives had changed. Although I'm sure waiting around wasn't easy for our parents, it was virtually impossible for us. Our impatience grew with each passing day. Finally, Hélène and I convinced our parents that it would be better for us to return to Paris where we could at least get jobs.

When we got back to Paris, we discovered that our brother Jacques and our brother-in-law Gaston, Aimée's husband, had both been drafted into the French army. This was a totally new experience for us, and in addition to the other changes, we now had to pray for their safety. Aimée lived in Melun, about thirty

BRENDA HANCOCK

minutes from Paris where she worked and cared for their daughter, Sylvianne. I didn't realize then how important it would be to have Aimée so close, yet at a "safe" distance.

Although we thought we were fairly grown up, Hélène and I still would not stay at the family apartment alone at night. Hélène had a best friend named Paulette, whose parents agreed to let us stay in their apartment each night so that we wouldn't be "unprotected" or vulnerable. So, while we looked for work, our parents remained in Cabourg with Robert and Madeleine, still waiting for whatever would happen next.

I shall never forget the morning of June 14, 1940. Paulette, Hélène, and I were walking down the Rue de Rivoli, heading from her apartment back to our own when we were approached by another friend, Annie. As we stood together in front of the Marie du Quatrieme (courthouse for the fourth district of Paris), she seemed to be speaking wildly, saying things that couldn't possibly be true. We all replied that she had to be crazy, that it was impossible that the Germans were pulling into Paris that very morning, but she kept insisting that they were only blocks away. Sure enough, it wasn't long before we heard the rumbling of trucks, and one by one a huge convoy rolled past us heading to the Hotel de Ville, the main city hall where all official papers were kept. We stood with many other Frenchmen in front of the Bazaar de L'Hotel de Ville (a large store) and cried as we watched the Germans pull down the French flag and raise the swastika. Hélène and I might not be official French citizens, but France was the only country we had known, and it cut us just as deeply as it did all the true Frenchmen surrounding us to see the symbol of our land being replaced. It just couldn't be happening to our country, not in our city.

Once the swastika was totally raised, there was no denying that life would soon be very different for us all. As we started to walk along the Rue de Rivoli heading back home, Hélène noticed that one of the trucks held French prisoners of war who were being guarded by German soldiers with big rifles. True to form, Hélène, who did not fear the devil himself, pushed past the guard and approached the Frenchmen on the truck, offering them cigarettes and asking about them. Much to the amazement of not only Annie, Paulette, and myself, but all the other Frenchmen on the street that day, the soldiers guarding the prisoners did not even say anything to Hélène as she interacted with the prisoners. Seeing this, the Frenchmen in the streets ran into stores to buy wine, bread, cigarettes, whatever they could think of to offer the prisoners. Annie, Paulette, and I joined Hélène, writing down names and addresses and promising to write "home" for these men to let their families know that they were alive. It may not have been much, but it felt very good to be defying these invaders of our country, even if only in a small way. We stayed until we had the names and addresses of all the prisoners and assured them that we would contact their families as soon as possible. We had no idea where these men would be taken or what their fate might be, but at least we could assure their families that they were safe on that one day and pass along the messages of love as they asked us to do.

After the trucks rolled away, heading to some unknown destination, the four of us headed back to our apartment where we found paper and pens and spent the rest of the day writing letters. It would have been nice to be able to tell these people that their son, husband, brother would be home soon, but just being able to give them what little information we could felt very rewarding. If it weren't for Hélène's independent, fearless nature, the families of those men would have remained clueless as to the whereabouts and health of their relative. That was not the first time I was very proud of my big sister, but it served to reinforce my admiration for her and her bravery. If only I could have had half of her courage, I would have been very happy.

BRENDA HANCOCK

CHAPTER 3

A Narrow Escape

Within two weeks of the Germans' arrival in Paris, our parents and younger siblings were back at the apartment with Hélène and me. They had heard of the "invasion" and wanted the family to be together. I suppose my parents somehow thought they could protect their children if only they were in the same city with us. For a while, life seemed to return to some semblance of normalcy.

One of the first radical changes came in 1941 when we were told that we had to go register as Jews. We all went down to the mairie (courthouse) and signed up, not even remotely realizing the implications of that action. By 1942 we were also made to wear a yellow star of David on our clothing so that we could be identified on sight. Next came the curfews. All Jews had to be off the streets by eight o'clock at night and had to remain indoors until six o'clock in the morning. Anyone found breaking curfew would be immediately arrested.

Being young and interested in having fun in whatever way we could, my siblings and I along with our many friends adapted. Instead of going to the movies from which we were banned, we would gather in each other's apartments, play records, and dance. Following French custom, the guests would bring wine and food so that we always managed to have plenty of refreshments to enjoy along with the music.

For a while life was almost normal. I worked with my father at the machines while Hélène worked outside the home and then went to her acting lessons. Madeleine and Robert went to school during the day, and Robert continued with his art lessons. Defiant as usual, Hélène would barely make it home before curfew most evenings. We always worried that there would come a night when she would be late and get into real trouble, primarily because of her defiant nature that would cause her to give whoever tried to arrest her a piece of her mind. Each night as she breezed in with seconds to spare, we all breathed a sigh of relief.

After working with my father for a while, I finally found a job working outside the home. Having heard that Dr. Etienne Albert, an obstetrician/gynecologist, needed a receptionist/assistant, I applied and was hired. My duties included greeting the patients, sterilizing instruments, making appointments, taking care of paperwork, anything in the office that could make Dr. Albert's job easier. He was a very kind man and a pleasant boss, which helped to make my job really enjoyable—much better than working at the machines with my father. Little did I know that it would be Dr. Albert's kindness that would save my life.

At the end of the workday on July 16, 1942, Dr. Albert, a Catholic with no fears for his own safety, came to me and said that he had heard there would be a raid after curfew that night to round up Jews in Paris. He suggested that I go home and get one of my sisters to come stay with me at the office for the night in order to be safe. Rushing home, I told my mother what Dr. Albert had said, and she immediately agreed with his plan. I wanted my sister Hélène to go with me, not only because, like me, she was not French, but I knew her bravery would carry us through the night. As usual, Hélène was not home. We waited as long as we possibly could before curfew would catch us out on the streets and truly vulnerable. Finally, my mother said that Madeleine should go with me and sent us along with warnings to be careful. We wouldn't find out until after curfew the next morning how costly Hélène's habit of barely beating curfew would be.

Early on the morning of July 17, Robert came rushing to Dr. Albert's office to tell Madeleine and me that Hélène had been taken and that I could not come home because they had asked for me, as well. Madeleine and I were in a state of shock and listened, not wanting to believe all that Robert had to say. Hélène had come in just moments before curfew with no time to join Madeleine and me at Dr. Albert's. Not long after, there was a knock at the door. Answering the menacing knock, my mother saw not German officials, but French policemen asking specifically for Hélène and me. As "indeterminees" or people without a country, we were among the first to be deported. Had we been French citizens, we could have appealed to our government for protection. Even being born in Poland didn't really give us the protection of the Polish government. Since we had lived almost our entire lives in France, Poland did not claim us as citizens either. At any rate, it turned out that the first round-ups were of people like Hélène and me who had no country.

Bold as ever, Hélène came to the door, told them who she was, and said she had no idea where I was, that I had not come home the night before. After making sure no one else in the apartment knew where I was, they told Hélène to get ready to leave. Three times, Hélène had an opportunity to escape, but she refused to go, fearful that she would put our parents and the rest of the family at risk if she did. Her first chance came when she asked if she could go around the corner for some things she would need. The policeman told her she could, but that she would need to hurry back. Gathering some paper and magazines from a neighborhood store, Hélène came back to the apartment to pack a few clothes, missing her chance at freedom.

Once she was downstairs with the others being rounded up, one of the French policemen came to her and offered her his apartment key, saying he would look the other way so she could escape. Once again, she refused this opportunity to be free. Looking coldly at the policeman, she said, "Why should I trust you who came to arrest me? Keep your key!" Even if she doubted the sincerity of his actions, she could have just walked away, not going to his apartment. Protecting her family was more important to her than her own freedom.

Her last chance to escape came when Madeleine heard that those taken were being held at a nearby school. She went to take Hélène some gloves and a scarf our mother thought Hélène might need. Upon arrival at the school, Madeleine told them she was a French citizen and needed to go in to see someone. They let her pass without even asking for papers. When she found Hélène, she tried to convince her to leave with her. They had been so lenient when Madeleine came in that she was sure they would have no problem leaving together. Again Hélène refused, telling Madeleine that she would do nothing that might jeopardize the rest of the family and assuring her that she would be fine. None of us ever saw Hélène again, nor did we hear anything more about her until after the war.

As for me, once Robert had come to the office and said I could not come home, Dr. Albert, who had just arrived in time to hear what had happened, asked if I had any family nearby where I could go for a while. When I told him my sister Aimée lived in Melun, he instructed me to tear the yellow star off my jacket. Once all signs of the emblem were gone, he took me to the train station, bought a one-way ticket to Melun, and saw me safely aboard the train before returning to his office for the day's work. All the way to Melun, all I could think of was Hélène's being

My beloved sister Hélène.

taken, of her being gone. How could this happen to my beautiful, brave, older sister whom I adored? When would I see her again? For that matter, when would I see my parents and other siblings? Even though I was nineteen years old, I was a very young, naïve nineteen, not ready to be thrust out into a very cold, cruel world.

When I arrived in Melun, I mechanically followed my feet to the shop where my sister worked, knowing she would be at work at that time of the day. I'm sure she thought I was babbling as I told her what had happened to Hélène and why I was there. She gave me the key to her apartment, and I went there and cried myself to sleep trying to erase the memories of that terrifying day. For the moment I was safe, but what was happening to Hélène? For that matter, what was going to happen to all of us? If they could take Hélène, what would keep them from taking us all?

CHAPTER 4

Thrust from the Nest

Life in Melun seemed to drag by. During the day I would play with my little niece, Sylvianne, while my sister would work. At night we would sit together and wonder what was going on in the world outside that apartment. We had no way of communicating with our parents, of finding out if they had any news from Hélène. After about a week of this, I could stand no more. Aimée agreed that I should try to go home and gave me the money for the train fare.

When I arrived back at our apartment, my mother hugged and kissed me, so very glad to see me again, and I held onto her as well. Surely, there would be safety in my mother's arms. Since I was there, Mother felt there had to be a plan for my safety. Who knew when they would come back asking for me again? Upstairs, Madame Shuster was an old widow who lived alone. She agreed that I could spend the nights at her apartment, hoping that no one would knock at her door searching for me. During the day I stayed in our apartment with our parents and again helped my father at the machines to pass the time. Every time there was a knock at the door, we would all jump in fear that they had come for me again. Nights weren't much easier as I sat with Madame Shuster and tried hard not to listen to every noise in the building. Not only was it taking a toll on me, but I could also see the strain my presence (or perhaps the fear of my being taken from them like Hélène had been) was putting on my parents.

We only endured several days of this tension before we decided there had to be another plan. My nephew Marcel, who was my age, and his sister-in-law's cousin Paulette were planning on leaving Paris and heading toward unoccupied France where they might find safety. They agreed that I should come along. Although I had never met Paulette, she was instrumental in saving my life. Her best friend, a Catholic girl named Pierette Nicodem, gave Paulette her birth certificate to give to me. Everyone in France had to have identity papers, and those who were Jews had "Juif" stamped on their papers. Marcel had managed to get false papers without the Jewish stamp because he had a friend who worked in the identification department, but only with papers for men. Paulette, too, already had papers that she felt would keep her safe. I was the only one without those needed documents until Paulette handed me that valuable birth certificate. We agreed that we would leave Paris on August 4, 1942.

On the evening of August 4, Paulette and Marcel met at our apartment to make final preparations for the trip. We all made sure none of our clothes had the yellow Star of David emblem on them. Trying to seem like students on a trip, we only took one change of clothes in a school satchel. About 7:30 that evening my mother walked us to the bridge called the Pont de Tournelle. Standing by the statue of Saint Geneviève on the bridge, my mother first kissed my nephew Marcel. Then she came to me, hugged me, kissed me, and told me to take care of myself. The plan was to let her know when I had reached safety, and she would send me more clothes and money to help me along. I think if I had realized that would be the last time I would ever see my

Paulette, who escaped Paris with me and gave me Pierette Nicodem's birth certificate.

Nephew Marcel Kuchman, who escaped Paris with me.

mother, nothing could have made me leave. As it was, I thought this was the only way to take away the tension I brought to the apartment just by being there and fearing the authorities who would come to take me away.

Optimistically, we three set off for the train station, the Gare d'Austerlitz, where we bought tickets to Bordeaux, still in occupied France. The trip to Bordeaux seemed to last through the night, with our sleep interrupted at each stop the train made. Fear gripped us each time the train stopped, and we prayed that the Germans wouldn't stop us and ask for papers since all I had was the birth certificate. The others might be under suspicion just by being with someone without papers. Finally, safely in Bordeaux we left the train station and headed to the bus station where we bought tickets to Darck, a small town on the border between occupied and unoccupied France. Marcel had been told a contact could be made in a café there. Once on the bus, we went to empty seats near the back, which turned out to be very lucky for us. Before the bus left, German officials boarded and began checking papers. I hoped the fear I felt was not expressed in my face, because if they came all the way to the back, we were lost. I, for sure, would be taken, and my traveling companions were at risk just for being with me. Time seemed to stand still as I waited for the worst to befall us. Amazingly, after checking just the first few rows, the Germans got off and let the bus depart. Marcel turned to me and said, "Well, I guess it just wasn't our day, huh?"

The remainder of the trip to Darck was uneventful—no more stops by Germans wanting to check papers, no one looking suspiciously at us. Despite the peacefulness of the ride through the countryside, fear was our constant companion. When the bus finally stopped in Darck, we took a deep breath, said silent prayers that our luck would still be with us, and went to look for the café Marcel had heard about from his friends. Since Darck was a small town, finding the café was not difficult at all. We went inside and ordered something to drink so that we could sit and watch carefully for a while before making a move that might be the end of us. When most of the customers had left, Marcel went up to the man at the counter to ask about getting help to cross to the unoccupied zone. It was a big risk, but we had no other options. Paulette and I sat warily watching the conversation and hoping for the best. Marcel walked back to our table to let us know the man had said to return at 5:00 that evening and someone would be there to help us. We left the café and wandered around the town, discussing the possibilities. On the one hand, this could very well be a trap that would send us all to our doom. Then again, we really had no other alternative. Time seemed to drag, and we all wished 5:00 would hurry so that the uncertainty would end.

At 5:00 we returned to the café and the man behind the

BRENDA HANCOCK

counter introduced us to two young men who would help us get to freedom for a price. We sat at a table where they made plans with us. First, they told us it would cost us five hundred francs which they wanted up front. Marcel refused to give them the entire amount, and they agreed to take half now and the other half when we were safe. Since they had to make some plans of their own, have dinner with their families or something like that, they told us they would return at 7:00 and we would depart then. Once again, we had time to kill during which we ate dinner and talked quietly about whether these men were the real thing or whether once more we had put ourselves at risk.

At 7:00, true to their word, the two men returned to the café and told us to follow them. Leaving the café, we walked for what seemed an unbelievable amount of kilometers without saying much at all. Finally, we arrived at a farm where the men told us to wait while they went up to the farmhouse. They talked quietly with the man who answered the door and then showed us to the barn. The farmer told us we could stay there for the night and that we had better get some rest because early the next morning we would need to be physically ready for the next step. Very early the next morning the farmer returned with coffee and wished us luck.

We walked again for quite some time before the young men stopped us. They said that we needed to form a line and lock arms with a man on each side of Paulette and myself. Once we had done this, they told us we would have to run and not stop running until they signaled that it would be OK to stop. The men and Marcel would try to make sure that Paulette and I could keep up with them by holding our arms and not letting us fall or stop for any reason. They asked us if we were ready, and then we began to run. With few trees to hide us, we ran through the countryside, crossed a highway, and continued running across fields. It seemed forever that we ran with my legs aching and my lungs burning with the need for air and rest, but finally the boys stopped and said, "You're safe. You're free." It seemed a miracle as Marcel gladly passed over the remaining fee. We thanked them over and over. They then told us they couldn't stay long because they had to get back before the Germans would be making rounds. As we bid them goodbye, we all three realized how very much we owed to these two wonderful young men. Unfortunately, we never even knew the names of these two heroes who had saved our lives.

CHAPTER 5

A New Life on My Own

Before they had left, the two young men who had taken us to freedom pointed the direction to the nearest town. Once we had rested some, we took off in the direction indicated and before long arrived in the small town of St. Angere. We knew the first order of business would be to get official papers for me. At the gendarmerie or police station, I went in to see if I could get that necessary document, an identity card without the stamp "Juif." Telling the man inside that I was on my way to Pau and had lost my papers along the way, I asked if I could get a replacement if I still had my birth certificate. The very nice man gave me temporary papers and said when I arrived at Pau, I could get my official papers there. Once I had the temporary document, we went to the bus station and bought tickets to Pau. Since Pau was the closest large city and a cousin, Anna, lived there, we had chosen this destination before leaving Paris.

After an uneventful bus ride we arrived in Pau, where the three of us went to Anna's apartment. Even though she had not been expecting us, she welcomed us with open arms and listened intently as we told her about Hélène and all the things going on in Paris, explaining our decision to go to the unoccupied zone. I showed her my new temporary papers and explained that the first thing I planned to do the next morning was get the official identity card. After that first night, Marcel decided to leave for Corez where his brother Jean and Jean's wife, Mariette, were living. He asked me if I wanted to go with him, but I decided to stay in Pau. Not only was Anna there, but I knew of several others from our neighborhood who were in town as well. After breakfast, Paulette left with Marcel, intending to join some members of her family who were not far away.

The first order of business for me was getting the official papers that would inconclusively change me from Cecile Widerman to Pierrette Nicodem. Once at the police station, I had no difficulty getting my papers, the temporary papers from St. Angere paving the way smoothly for my transformation. Since I was no longer a Jewish girl from Paris, I knew it would be best for me to go to a hotel to stay, rather than remain with Anna and her family. Fortunately, I had a little money left from what my parents had given me—crossing to safety hadn't taken it all.

Luck was still with me as I walked through the streets of Pau in search of inexpensive housing and wondered what I would do next. I found a small hotel where I rented a room, knowing I would have to find work soon in order to be able to remain on my own. After checking out the room, I decided just sitting around in this small space wouldn't accomplish anything. I had to find a way to support myself until I could hear from my mother. Walking along the streets of Pau and wondering exactly what I should do, I was surprised to meet a friend from home. Although I knew she and her family were in Pau, I had no idea where they lived and again realized how lucky I was to run into her on the streets. My friend took me back to her house where I was warmly welcomed by her entire family. Not only did they feed me a wonderful dinner, but they also knew of a job I could possibly get. They had heard of a lady whose husband was a prisoner of war. Because she was alone, she needed someone to take care of her two small boys while she worked. The job didn't pay much, but it would provide room and board, which was basically all I would need until I could hear from my parents who had promised to send along more clothes once I was safe. I gladly took the address and went the next day for an interview. Madame Gerard proved to be the lifeline I needed.

Within two days life had settled down to a comfortable routine. While Madame Gerard went to work, I watched over Pierre and Claud, aged two and four. Since I had grown up in an apartment full of children, taking care of her two sweet little boys was fairly easy. I had my own room, and fortunately for me all Madame Gerard wanted me to do was watch the children. I didn't have to clean or cook, which was lucky for her since I had never even boiled water before. However, even this peaceful life didn't last very long.

One day in early October I was walking in the street with the two little boys when I was surprised to see my sister Madeleine coming toward me. Instead of having good news and extra clothes, she shocked me with the news that "everyone" had been taken on September 23, 1942. My sister Ida, her husband, Jacques, and their sons Bernard and Edmond had been in the apartment with our parents when the authorities arrived. Madeleine had a little warning and told our mother she refused to go with them and would find some place to hide. Madame Zilberbert, a very close friend, had given my mother the key to her apartment two stories above ours before she was taken on the same day as my sister, Hélène. Mother took the key and gave it to Madeleine, telling her to take Robert with her to hide in the restroom. Quickly, Madeleine took the key, kissed Mother goodbye, and tried to make Robert come with her. Not wanting to be left alone with his sister who was just seventeen months older than he, Robert insisted on staying with the family. Deciding there was no way to convince him to come with her, Madeleine went upstairs, locked herself in the restroom of the apartment, and waited. Twice Robert went upstairs to take money and the key to our apartment to Madeleine before the authorities forced everyone who was Jewish in the building to leave. Madeleine waited throughout the night in the restroom, listening carefully to any sounds that might indicate someone was still looking for her. The next morning she went to our brother Jacques, who went back with her to our apartment to try to retrieve a few of our things. The concierge told them on that last visit that they could not return to the apartment, so Madeleine stayed with Jacques for a few days, trying to decide what to do. Finally deciding to leave Paris, also, she had stopped in Pau to see if she could find me to let me know what had happened. She planned to go on to Marseilles to find Henri, Madame Zilberbert's oldest son, to see if she could stay with him and find work. She had no clothes for me, only a little money to share in case I wanted to leave Pau as well, and nothing more except the horrible news that everyone was gone. In what seemed like a flash, she was gone, and I was walking mechanically back to Madame Gerard's house, wondering what my next move should be.

CHAPTER 6

Off to Marseilles

A week after Madeleine had come, I decided I should also go to Marseilles. I wasn't sure where Madeleine was, but she was the only family I had left, and I just thought we should be together. Taking the money I had saved from my job along with what Madeleine had given me, I thanked Madame Gerard as I said goodbye to her and the two boys and bought a ticket for the train to Marseilles. My mind whirled as the train made its way across the French countryside, and I barely noticed the beauty of the landscape and how different the countryside was from the places I had known all my life. So many things had already changed for me, and now there would be even more. I'd never been to Marseilles before, but it wasn't as big as Paris, so surely I could find my way around and figure out what to do when I got there—at least, that's what I tried to convince myself of as the train made its way southward.

Once in Marseilles, I realized that finding Madeleine was not going to be so easy. I had no idea where Henri Zilberbert lived or even if Madeleine was still with him. All I could do was walk the streets, looking for another small hotel that would not be too expensive and hoping that luck would still be with me and help me know what the next step should be. As I think back on what happened during those life-changing days, I am constantly amazed at how many times luck, coincidence, whatever you want to call it, played a part in my survival.

Walking aimlessly through the streets of Marseilles in search of an inexpensive hotel, I saw on the street coming toward me an acquaintance from Paris. Her cousins had lived in our apartment building, and we'd visited often when she came to see them. After our first happy greetings, I erased the happiness by sharing with her all that Madeleine had told me. Not only had my family been taken on September 23, but her cousins as well, according to Madeleine. Until that moment, she had no idea of what had happened in Paris. She had not seen Madeleine and did not know where I might find either her or Henri Zilberbert, but she took me back to the hotel where she was staying with her family so that I could have supper with them and gather my thoughts about what to do next rather than just wander the streets. During supper, someone told me that they'd seen an advertisement in the newspaper for someone to take care of a child. They still had the newspaper there, so I knew from the advertisement I was to go to a jewelry store and ask for Madame Pollack, who turned out to be the grandmother of the child needing a caretaker.

Even though I went to the jewelry store as soon as possible, the grandmother—Madame Pollack—told me that the job had already been taken. Her daughter and son-in-law were both lawyers whose work made it necessary for them to have a nanny, but someone had applied and received the job before I got there. I fearfully wondered if perhaps my luck had run out. Although I didn't want to appear desperate, I asked Madame Pollack if she knew of any other jobs that might be available since I really needed to find work as soon as possible. She was such a kind lady,

BRENDA HANCOCK

and I still don't know what it was about me that made her feel she could trust me or made her want to help, but she explained that there was an option I could take. Telling me that her own husband was sick and needed to go to the country to recuperate, she said she could use someone to watch over her home while they were gone. The job would not involve any actual pay, but it would give me a place to live and food every day. With the Germans in the north and no one certain of what would happen next, she didn't feel comfortable leaving the house unoccupied. I thankfully accepted her offer and breathed a sigh of relief. As long as I had food and shelter, I really didn't need any money—at least not for a while anyway.

Before arriving at the home, I had no idea of what to expect, but even my wildest imaginations had never envisioned the huge house she showed me as hers. Not only was I amazed at its size— it filled half a city block—but I could hardly believe that each bedroom had its own bath. We had considered ourselves lucky that our apartment had its own toilet and that the public bathhouse where we took our showers was just downstairs from our apartment. This house was unbelievably beautiful and exquisitely furnished, but I was further awed when Madame Pollack showed me to her son's room and told me it would be mine while I stayed there since he was currently a prisoner of war. She was taking me into her home as if I were one of her children. I was certain I had been sent an angel in the form of this wonderful little lady. All I had to do was be there, not all the time, but at least to make it evident someone lived there so there would be no vandalism. What an amazing lady this was and what an incredible job—to live like a princess in such beautiful surroundings! Although Monsieur and Madame Pollack did move to the country, she would still come into town to work at the jewelry store, so I had ample opportunity to get to know and care greatly about this guardian angel who had come into my life.

By November of 1942, the Germans had managed to occupy all of France, so being Pierrette Nicodem was doubly important to me. I guarded my identity papers carefully and immersed myself into my new non-Jewish life, trying hard not to think too much about my dear sister Hélène, about my parents and the rest of my family who were lost to me. I had no idea where they might be, what they might be doing, or even if they were still alive. All I could do was live day to day and hope that one day the nightmare would go away. Granted, my surroundings and my current circumstances ensured that I was quite comfortable physically, and few would think of that existence as a nightmare. Yet, every day was filled with a nagging fear that someone would discover who I was and take me away, combined with the worries about my family and what the future might hold for us all. As for Madeleine, my younger sister who had been too self-involved as we grew up for me to be really close to her like I was with Hélène, I didn't even see or get to spend time with her. Being blonde with blue eyes as well as a native Frenchwoman, she didn't risk being pulled aside and asked for papers as other Jews who actually "looked" like the stereotypical Jew. Not as headstrong as Hélène, Madeleine still had that air about her that made me feel she was managing just fine, wherever she was. I hoped I was right.

Even after the Germans had occupied all of France, I still had several months of comfort at Madame Pollack's amazing house before once again having to make a move. Once the Germans had established themselves in Marseilles, they decided Madame Pollack's palatial house would be perfect for them. Answering a knock at the door, I was met by more German soldiers than I ever cared to see. Fortunately, at least one of them spoke French and was able to inform me of their intentions. Pushing past me, they came into the residence, already acting as if it belonged to them. They told me to gather my things and leave as this was now to be their headquarters. Not nearly as brave as Hélène, I didn't yell in their faces that they had no right even to set foot in this house, but I did try to protest at least a little and tell them that the house belonged to Monsieur and Madame Pollack, not them. I soon learned that these German soldiers were not the passive ones we had encountered that first day in Paris when Hélène had pushed her way past them to talk to the French prisoners. Not only were they not passive, they soon became aggressive, and I found myself on the receiving end of a forceful ejection from the house. My few possessions and I were strewn and sprawled in the street as I was literally kicked out of this beautiful place I had called home. As I picked up my few scattered belongings, the thought crossed my mind that I should be thankful that the not-so-gentle shove was the worst I had to experience from them. It seemed that possession was the law, and they demanded possession of that house. There was nothing I could do except go to the jewelry store in the hopes that Madame Pollack was there so that I could tell her what had happened.

That amazing woman seemed more concerned with my welfare than with what was happening to her home. Like a mother hen, she checked to make sure I was not physically hurt while she assured me that I had nothing to worry about, that she was already figuring out where I could go now that the house was no longer available. She had another daughter, Odette Carcasonne, who was the divorced mother of two sons who were off at school. Madame Carcasonne proved to be as nice as her mother, giving me her sons' room and telling me I could stay there as long as I needed. She would be gone during the days since she worked at a dentist's office, and I could spend my time however I wished. Once again, I was treated as a member of the family and not asked to do any housework or anything else to repay them for their hospitality. During the days I would roam the streets aimlessly, ending up at the dentist's office by the time Madame Carcasonne was ready to go home. We would walk back to her apartment together where

Me as Pierrette with Mme Vidal (friend of Mme Carcasonne) and Mme Carcasonne on the way to church in Marseilles.

she would prepare dinner for the two of us. In return for all of this, I kept my room clean—nothing more was asked of me.

After going daily to meet Madame Carcasonne at the dentist's office for several weeks, I was surprised one day when the dentist asked if she could speak privately with me. I followed her into the office, at first wary and fearful that somehow she had discovered my secret and I was once again in danger. Imagine my surprise when instead of wanting to turn me in to the Germans, she asked me if I was interested in helping France. Without hesitation, I answered affirmatively. Once she was assured of my sincerity, she

BRENDA HANCOCK

explained that I could work with the Forces Françaises de l'Interieur, the French Underground. They were in need of couriers, and my job would be to carry messages and sometimes ammunition and guns. I would travel by bicycle from Marseilles to the surrounding small towns to carry out these important tasks. She warned me that it was dangerous, that if I were caught, it would most likely mean certain death. At this point in my life, not knowing if I even had any family left, I really didn't care about my life. Anything I could do to help get rid of the Germans, to try to return France to the way it used to be before they came, would be worth whatever the cost. She told me she would be in touch.

CHAPTER 7

Missions with the FFI

Since I didn't have a job, it was fairly easy for me to carry out the missions that were asked of me. My first missions were carried out during the day when most other people were working. For my very first mission, the dentist, Madame Pendariez, called me to her office where she introduced me to a man who would go with me to show me how things were done. Names were not exchanged, with the explanation that the less I actually knew, the better it would be. If I happened to be stopped or caught, there would be nothing I could tell them. Even if they tortured me, I could not disrupt the Underground or give away the identity of any Underground members, other than Madame Pendariez, who had first asked me to participate. I'm certain she knew I would rather die than risk her life or the life of Madame Carcasonne, who also knew I had accepted this challenge.

My first mission was fairly simple. I had a message that gave the specifics about a train carrying ammunition—where it would be and when to blow it up. In order to introduce me to my contact and make certain the delivery would go smoothly, the stranger walked me through this first mission. He had two bicycles for us to use to get to the small town where the contact would be made. In the future this same bicycle would be my mode of transportation from Marseilles to the surrounding villages where I would meet my contact. It was a good thing I was young and had spent so much time just walking around the streets. That exercise had prepared me well for these extended rides to the countryside. As we rode along that first day, he explained to me that there was always going to be a chance that the Germans would stop me to ask for my papers and to question the reasons for my traveling. Should this happen while he was with me, all I should do was show my papers and let him do the talking. Once I was on my own, again I was to show my papers willingly and act like nothing was out of the ordinary, telling them I was going to the next town to visit relatives. He explained that my youthful, innocent appearance would most likely allow me to get through any questioning the Germans might make if I were stopped in the future when I went on missions alone. When we actually were stopped that day, I learned the miracle of identity papers with no "Juif" stamped on them. After a brief look at our papers and a simple explanation from the stranger, we were waved on without being frisked or even having them search through my school satchel where the message was hidden. Although my heart was pounding so that I was certain the Germans could hear it, apparently he was right about my appearance causing them no suspicion. I must admit that I looked younger than my age since I wore no makeup and was indeed quite näive. Who would suspect a girl of fourteen or fifteen (as I obviously looked) carrying out sabotage against the enemy? Certainly, they didn't—not then and, fortunately for me, not ever during any of my missions.

Once in the small village, the stranger introduced me to my contact—again without our exchanging names. If I were to deliver messages in the future, it would be only to this tall, slender man with brown hair that was turning gray at the temples or to someone who was with him. Never would I be asked to pass a message to someone I had never seen before. In this way, I could be more readily assured of my safety, and the actual fighting members of the Underground would be assured they were not being tricked into something that would result in their capture. Passing the message was amazingly easy, and all the way home I had an unbelievable sense of accomplishment, a feeling I had actually done something worthwhile for a change. Not only would the completion of a mission result in my breathing a sigh of relief that I hadn't been caught, but every mission after that first one also brought that great feeling of satisfaction, of feeling that somehow I was pouring salt into a German wound, paying them back bit by bit for the disruption they had caused to my life. It was a good thing the next day that I was alone listening to the radio when the report of a train being blown up was given. Anyone in the room would have wondered at the great joy that exploded over my face as I realized that my message from England had been properly passed along and that in a small way I had helped to blow up that train. After that first experience, I learned to train my expression to hide the joy I felt inside when news of my efforts came over the radio.

Two days passed before I was sent on a second mission, this time alone. I have to admit that the ride to that small village where I was to meet my contact was filled with my imagination running wild. On the one hand, I felt this great exhilaration at being given such a huge responsibility. At the same time, I feared that somehow I would let everyone down, that I would do something to jeopardize the entire operation. I tried to think of only pleasant, happy thoughts so that my face would give nothing away, focusing on the beauty of the day, the green countryside around me and how peaceful it all seemed despite the war that was being waged all around us. When I was stopped by the Germans, I simply handed over my papers, briefly answered that I was going to the village to visit my grandmother, smiled, and thanked them as they sent me along my way. It seemed that, like my brother and sister, I was an actress—maybe not good enough to perform on stage, but good enough to stay alive and cause no suspicions. Once in the village, my contact was exactly where I was told he would be, and I passed the message along, feeling as if a great weight had been lifted from me. That day he told me I could call him Phillippe—that it wasn't his real name, but that would be the name I would use with him or to anyone else he might send me to for passing along information. I would tell the new person that Phillippe had sent me. Then he asked me for a name—not my real one, but one he could use. That's when I decided my "code" name would be Nick—short for Nicodem. I was still barely used to being Pierette, and now I was Nick. As I left, he said, "Good-bye, Little Nick." Petite Nick, that was how they referred to me from then on, and it probably fit well since I not only looked very young but also was an inch or two under five feet tall. The ride back to Marseilles, unlike the one to the village, was filled only with exhilaration, with a sense of great accomplishment. I had successfully completed my first mission alone.

By early 1943 even this pleasant existence of having no responsibilities other than running a mission a couple of times a week was changed. Madame Carcasonne was told that she would have to give up her apartment and find some other place to live. Even under the stress of having to find a new home, this kind and generous lady offered to move into an apartment large enough for me to continue living with her. Although I felt safe and comfortable with her, I realized that staying with her might end up endangering her if I were ever caught. I was also tired of endlessly roaming the streets and doing nothing more than existing. I needed to find work and begin supporting myself, but where could I go? What kind of work could I do?

Once again I was extremely lucky in finding a new situation.

The lady who took over Madame Carcasonne's apartment introduced me to her daughter, who was a ballet dancer. This lovely young lady took me under her wing, as so many before her had done, and took me to a Catholic home for girls that she knew of in the city. Not only did she make me aware of the facility, but she also paid for my first month's stay there. This place was similar to the YWCA that one finds in America, a large building where young girls could live safely. In actuality, there were two separate buildings, one set aside for the nuns who ran the place and the other for the young girls. Many of the girls there had come from the surrounding countryside to find work. Since everything was rationed, often there was not enough food for an entire family, which forced these young women to go to the larger cities to find work and a way to support themselves. Although everyone there worked for a living, the routine also included the residents' mandatory attendance at daily prayers. I very quickly had to immerse myself in Catholicism, learning the prayers and customs of that religion and embracing them as my own, at least for appearance's sake.

In addition to paying for my first month's rent, this delicate ballerina also introduced me to Monsieur Pianelli, the boss of a mineral water warehouse, who hired me to work as his secretary. For the first time, I felt I was actually on my own, a responsible adult and not just another protected member of a family. Although Monsieur Pianelli was a small, rather stooped, stern-looking man, he proved to be a wonderful boss. It wasn't long before my hard work made him feel he could trust me even more than his own lazy son, who also worked at the warehouse. I was surprised the first time he asked me to accompany his son to make the deposits at the bank. As it turned out, Monsieur Pianelli didn't trust his son very much and felt he could unhesitatingly trust me. Soon, I was making the daily deposits on my own and was so very proud of the trust Monsieur Pianelli had shown that I never failed him in this important part of my job.

Life took on a pleasant routine. Five days a week I would work for Monsieur Pianelli, earning enough money to pay for my rent at the home with some to spare for clothes (when I had ration coupons to buy some) or entertainment like the movies. About once or twice a week I would be asked to go on a mission, which by that time had become routine. Monsieur Pianelli let me leave early or even have the day off if I told him I wasn't feeling well or needed to go somewhere. Surprisingly, he never asked me questions and never wavered in his trust of me. I never knew if he knew the real reason for my "illnesses" and it was his sympathy with the cause against the Germans that made him so willing to let me leave early or take the day off or whether he just understood that I was not as healthy as I looked. At any rate, I managed to successfully carry out both my duties as his secretary and as a member of the Underground. Going on missions on the ride to the village, I no longer felt fear, just a sense of purpose, always accompanied by great satisfaction on the ride home, and Monsieur Phillippe was becoming a trusted, welcome acquaintance.

When I first moved into the Catholic home, I was placed in a room with Henriette, a girl also from Paris although I had never met her there, and two other girls, both named Jacqueline. One Jacqueline was blonde, while the other was a brunette, so we referred to them as Jacqueline la blonde and Jacqueline la

Henriette and me in Marseilles.

brune—at least until we figured out that Jacqueline la brune was a thief, at which point I called her Jacqueline the thief! Various things from small articles of clothing to soap to ration cards had been disappearing from our room, but we were not quite sure who was responsible.

The ration card situation seemed to be the key to the mystery. Each of the girls at the home was given ration cards for everything from food to clothing. We were allowed to keep the ration cards for bread and sugar, but the rest of the food coupons were given as part of our rent to the home in order for them to buy the food for the meals they provided. After the irritation of the other small things that had been taken, we were not the slightest bit amused to discover that even our sugar ration cards disappeared. Shortly after our discovery of their being missing, in walked Jacqueline la brune with a sack of cookies. I don't know if it was a result of losing my family or being in the Underground or just being on my own and having to take care of myself, but when I saw those cookies, I lost my usual sweet, quiet disposition, along with my temper. To her face, I called Jacqueline a thief. My demeanor must have been extremely threatening because she ran

Me on the balcony at the home.

to the lavatory and locked herself in. She didn't try to fight me or even deny my accusations, which led me to believe she truly had been the thief all along. Henriette, Jacqueline la blonde, and I all went Madame Perdeno, the directrice of the home, to explain that we no longer wanted Jacqueline la brune as our roommate. In her place, we asked if Suzanne Luga, a girl who lived in a room next to ours, could move in with us.

BRENDA HANCOCK

Under the circumstances, she and the nuns agreed to this change, opening the door to perhaps the best part of this new life, an amazing friendship that has continued for over sixty years.

Suzanne and Henriette on the balcony at the home where we waved at the bombers as they flew over.

CHAPTER 8

New Friends, New Challenges

Coming to work in Marseilles from a town called Montauban, Suzanne Luga was short like me, yet much more slender. Although small, she was like dynamite, full of energy and a sense of humor that helped return laughter to my world. Never before had I met someone who could find humor in even the most mundane things of everyday life. Suzanne and I shared our room, our clothes, our ration coupons, and eventually even our hopes and dreams. Henriette, Jacqueline, Suzanne, and I lived together in that one room, which was sparsely furnished with four single beds and one wardrobe in which to put our clothes. Most of us had a rather sparse wardrobe, so we naturally shared what we had, being especially careful of each other's clothes since even if you had money, you needed ration coupons in order to buy new ones. Although I had left Paris with only one change of clothes, I had managed to get a few more things. Madame Carcasonne had given me a nice outfit before I left her home, and a friend I had met in my early wanderings, a prostitute named Monique, who was very nice and kind despite her profession, gave me clothes from time to time.

Suzanne, me, and Monique, who befriended me in Marseilles and gave me clothes.

The only decorations were a crucifix that hung on one wall and some pictures that the other girls had brought with them. I had only one small photo of my brother, which I kept with me, but Suzanne had lots of pictures not only of her family, but also of movie stars, since she worked for a photographer. Those photos helped brighten the tiny space. The bathroom was a large facility down the hall that was shared by everyone on the floor.

Although the four of us shared everything from ration coupons to clothes, I felt closer to Suzanne than the other two. She could never replace Hélène in my heart, but she was more

Suzanne Luga in the room at the Catholic home for girls.

like a sister than a friend. At night when I would wake up from a nightmare about my family being gone, it was Suzanne who was there to comfort me, to assure me that I was safe and that one day life would be normal. The first time this happened was a very strange dream to me. There was an infinitely tall ladder that I was compelled to climb. Someone had told me that if I climbed the

BRENDA HANCOCK

ladder, I would find my family. Naturally, I began to climb, feeling more and more eager the higher I got. When I was about halfway up, my father appeared and said, "Where do you think you are going?" I told him that someone told me if I climbed up I would find where you are. To this he replied, "Where we are, you cannot come." I began to beg him to let me come, let me be with the rest of the family. He kept insisting that where they were, I could not come. It was then that I woke up sobbing with Suzanne kneeling by my bed comforting me. Another time she was there for me in the night was the day of my brother's eighteenth birthday. Again I had a dream, this time about him, and again I awoke to the sound of my own sobs and Suzanne's comforting voice assuring me life would once again be normal some day.

Suzanne was so much fun, having a unique ability to bring laughter back into my life. Her observations about the things we encountered every day along the way to work, to lunch, and back for supper were always amusing, causing us to spend a great deal of our walks laughing and giggling. Perhaps because we shared those walks, Suzanne and I were somehow a bit closer to each other than to the other two girls despite the fact that the four of us were always together and shared everything. The strange thing is that Suzanne turned out to be the only true Catholic in our room. Henriette and Jacqueline and I were all from Paris and all Jewish.

As for my missions, more often than not, I would receive word of an impending mission in the evening when we were in our room. Someone would yell up the staircase that I had a phone call. I would go down to hear the message that I was needed. Grabbing my school satchel that I had brought with me from Paris and some papers and books, I would go to the designated meeting place to receive the message that had come from England or to get the guns or ammunition that would need to be transported. If it was just a message, I would put it in my underwear or my pocket, knowing that if they searched the bag, they would surely find it. The school bag and books were a ruse that would verify that I was just a kid. Surely any Germans who stopped me would see the school books on top, find only papers and books, and let me go on my way without frisking me or searching in my clothes. When it was guns or ammunition instead of just a message, I would be given a special suitcase and ordered to take the train to meet my contact since I couldn't carry a suitcase on the bicycle. The contraband would be hidden underneath a special false bottom with clothes on top in the hope that if the Germans stopped and searched, they would be in a hurry and not look past the clothes. Fortunately for me, the plan worked every time.

Everything seemed to fall into a sort of routine with me until one weekend when Henriette asked me to accompany her to the Bas Alpes to visit her brother who was in the French Underground stationed there. First I had to verify with Monsieur Phillippe that I would not be needed for the weekend. I just asked him if I could go away for the weekend without any problems rather than let him know I was planning to visit someone in the Underground in the Alps. He said if something came up, they would find someone else to run the mission and wished me a pleasant weekend. Once everything was squared away, Henriette and I caught a train to the Alps. After arriving in the small town, Henriette had directions to go to the home of an older lady who turned out to be the person who always received and sent the letters between the two. We waited at her home while she went to the woods to meet Willie, Henriette's brother, and make arrangements for us to meet. Late in the evening, she came back with the news that we could follow her the next day into the woods to meet them. Even though it was very dangerous for them as well as us, we met in the woods a great distance from the town by foot. After traipsing deep into the woods, the old lady whistled in a peculiar way, and suddenly

BRENDA HANCOCK

Willie and two of his fellow Underground members appeared out of the woods. I could see how close their relationship was as soon as we met, since Henriette jumped into his arms and he swung her around, grinning and kissing her. When she introduced me, I was impressed with his beautiful smile. As we sat on the ground in the woods visiting, I saw that in addition to being handsome, he was smart and very nice. Before we left, he asked me if I would like to begin writing to him. When I said that sounded nice, he told me that I could send my letters through this lady and he would send responses to me through her as well. That began a great friendship that seemed to hold possibilities of much more. Not long after our meeting, Henriette was telling everyone that Willie and I were engaged, probably more from her wanting to have me as her sister-in-law than anything that Willie and I had ever said to each other. Although we never saw each other again until after I'd returned to Paris, he ended up sending a love song he had written to me in one of the letters he'd sent Henriette, probably encouraging her even more that one day we would be "sisters."

Eventually my trust in Suzanne was so complete that I even let her accompany me on a mission one time. She never actually knew that I was going on a mission that time, but I had a trip I needed to make to a neighboring village. This mission was farther, so we would need to ride a bus to the town where I was to deliver my important package. Before leaving the home, we had to be certain that we would return by 9 P.M. or sign a big book saying where we would be for the night. Fortunately for me, I had encountered a friend of my parents, a lady with whom they had become friends during their stay in Cabourg. She and her daughter and two sons had moved to Marseilles and invited me to come spend time with them whenever I wanted. After several visits, I asked this kind lady if she would cover for me should anyone call asking if I were there. Once she agreed, I always signed out that

I was going to visit with her and her children. Luckily, no one ever called her and caused her to have to lie for me. As I think back on it, I wonder that Suzanne never questioned these little trips, never came right out and asked me what on earth I was doing all those times I left for the evening or left for the weekend.

On this one particular occasion that I let Suzanne join me, I was sent to a town too far for the bicycle and given the name of an older woman at whose home I was supposed to stay. Since the mission required a bus trip and an overnight stay, Suzanne decided to go with me. Again, she did not know I was working for the Underground—only that I was going out of town for the week-end and going with me sounded like more fun than staying in Marseilles. We went to the bus station where we bought tickets and waited for our bus to arrive. Once aboard, I sat on one side of the bus and Suzanne sat across the aisle from me next to a young Frenchman with whom she began a conversation. After riding the bus for a while, we came into a small town where the bus driver told us we would stop for a short time. The young man asked Suzanne and me if we would like to accompany him to the small café across the street from where the bus stopped for a grena-dine. Suzanne eagerly said, "Yes," so I was left with nothing to do except follow. Leaving our luggage on the bus and taking only my purse with the message safely tucked in the bottom, we followed the young man to the café, expecting to return shortly and con-tinue on our way. Once inside, we were laughing, drinking our grenadines, and having a good time. Then suddenly I saw out the window that our bus was leaving without us. We raced to the doorway only to see the bus turn the corner out of sight. Never had I been so angry with Suzanne and her desire for a grenadine! The young man was very apologetic and assured us he would find transportation for us to get to our destination. With that, he left and I let Suzanne know exactly how upset I was with her. In just a little while, he returned with the news that he had found a man with a truck heading in the direction we needed who was willing to take us along as far as he could. Having no other options, we followed the young man around the corner where a man with a big truck was waiting. He said he could take us as far as Allemagne—not the country of Germany as it is called in France, but a small town near our destination. It seemed to be our only solution, so Suzanne and I sat in the front of the truck beside this driver with my anger at her barely dissipating. Before we got in the truck, we both noticed that the back of the truck was full of men, but we didn't ask any questions.

After riding in silence for quite a while (me because I was still so angry with Suzanne and Suzanne because she knew better than to talk to me when I was that upset), we heard one of the men in the back knock on the back window of the truck and call out, "Hey, Monsieur Petiot." Suzanne and I did not hear the rest of what the man had to say because we had both turned to each other and were staring with great fear into each other's eyes, wondering exactly what we had gotten ourselves into this time. Even before I had left Paris I had seen in the news the stories about Doctor Petiot that were enough to frighten even the most strong of heart. It seems that Mr. Petiot had promised many Jewish people that he would help them escape from France, telling them to bring along all their prized possessions and a certain amount for the fee. Once they arrived at his office, he would kill them, take their possessions and money, and incinerate the bodies so that his dastardly deeds would not be discovered. Some minor mistake in his plans had revealed his actions, and the news spread throughout France like wildfire. Once the news broke, he had disappeared. The man driving beside me fit the general description—he was the right age and once we heard his name, he even seemed to have a foreboding air about him. After hearing this man's name, we continued to ride in complete silence, but now each of us mulled over this new predicament and wondered how we would manage to survive this turn of events. My managing to complete this mission seemed to be less likely than ever.

Shortly after learning the man's name, we noticed that the truck was slowing down and turning into a lane that led to a farmhouse. Mr. Petiot turned to us after he had stopped the truck and asked if we were hungry. We both nodded that we were, afraid that he might be planning on fattening us up for the kill. Acknowledging our hunger, he handed us some ham and bread, and I immediately found the courage to ask him how he thought we could eat since we had no way to cut the food. He shrugged and handed me his knife before walking off to have a discussion with the farmer. Looking at the long blade of the knife, I whispered to Suzanne that I was not going to give it back and that if he tried to kill us, he'd get a taste of his knife first. For once, that bubbly, energetic girl that I knew Suzanne to be was nowhere to be seen. I don't know if it was the fear of Monsieur Petiot or hearing me threaten to kill someone that had silenced her, but not a word was spoken as we ate the meat and bread. Once the meal was finished, I hid his knife in the pocket of my jacket and kept my hand on it, ready to defend myself and Suzanne should the need occur.

In a little while Mr. Petiot returned to the truck, which he and the men loaded with supplies from the farm. When the load was secure and the men had gotten back into the truck, Mr. Petiot steered the truck away from the farm and deep into the surrounding woods. Again, Suzanne and I rode along in silence, each imagining the terrible fate that awaited us and praying that we would make it out of this alive. I kept my hand securely clutching the handle of the knife, telling myself that I *could* kill someone if it meant saving my life and that of my friend. Once we were deep in the woods, Mr. Petiot stopped the truck and turned to us. He looked even more menacing as he spoke in a voice that promised a fate even worse than his words suggested. I could

BRENDA HANCOCK

hardly believe my ears as I listened to his threats. It seemed that he was working with the Underground, delivering these men and supplies to a unit based in these woods. In the most threatening tone I had ever heard, he said, "You know where we are and what this is. If *anyone* finds out, I'll find **you**!" He assured us that if he heard of any harm coming to these men or any leak of information giving out the location of this group of Underground fighters, he would know it was the two of us who divulged the information and would make us pay dearly. Although I knew I could not give away my own part in the Underground, I breathed a sigh of relief as Suzanne and I promised him that we would never breathe a word to anyone. After the men and supplies were unloaded, Monsieur Petiot drove the truck on into Allemagne and bought a drink for Suzanne and me before bidding us good-bye. Before he left, I thanked him for all he had done and handed him back his knife, never letting him know that I was in the Underground, too, and carried information that was key to the success of a given mission.

When we left the café where Monsieur Petiot had bought us our drinks, we knew the only choice we had was to begin walking the seventeen kilometers to the next town, the site of our original destination. Strangely enough, there were absolutely no cars on the road that day—no French drivers, no German drivers, no one. As we walked, Suzanne and I marveled at our close call, laughing nervously at the thought that we could very well have been killed that afternoon. Suzanne even teased me about the knife and my threats of violence against the much larger and stronger Monsieur Petiot. Although our conversations made the walk seem not that far at all, we were both extremely tired before we were even halfway to our destination and I had to cajole and even sing to encourage Suzanne to continue walking until someone came along to give us a ride or until we actually got there. Unfortunately, no one ever came along and we trudged our way to the village. Much to our amazement, once we got to our destination, there sat our bus, complete with our possessions still waiting where we had left them earlier that day. We were so lucky that the bus had stopped for the night and would not leave again until morning. We grabbed our bags and made our way to the house of the old lady who was to be my contact.

Once at her house, I gave her the code word and she replied correctly with the expected response before inviting us in and showing us our rooms. I told Suzanne I'd be back in a little while, to wait for me there, and once she was out of earshot, the old lady told me where to go to deliver my message. I made it clear to the lady that Suzanne was not involved, didn't know anything, and that I wanted to keep her out of it to keep her safe. Since she understood my concern for my friend, she agreed that she would stay and entertain Suzanne until I got back. Not only did I complete my mission with ease, but once I returned I found the old lady to be quite a marvel. Suzanne and I relaxed and enjoyed spending the rest of the day with her before returning to Marseilles. As we walked in the village with her before we left, some friends from the village greeted her and asked who her company was. She smiled and replied that we were her nieces! Suddenly, this lady who had lived in the village and known these people all her life had nieces! I was pleased to be able to visit the little old lady who was now my "aunt" again several times on missions before I left Marseilles.

CHAPTER *9*

Problems in Marseilles

As I said earlier, it turned out that Suzanne was the only true Catholic in our room. Eventually, I learned that Henriette and Jacqueline were from the eighteenth arrondisement in Paris, a place everyone knew was inhabited primarily by Jewish families. Living on Rue des Deux Ponts, I was in the fourth arrondisement that was not known to be a center for Jews, even though there was an area called the Pletzl of Paris in which all the inhabitants were Jewish. Our building on Ile St. Louis was the only one with Jewish families, so they didn't immediately suspect I was Jewish as I suspected they were. Eventually, Suzanne knew that the three of us were Jewish—the only Jews in the entire building. Jacqueline's parents had never spoken Yiddish, only French, but Henriette and I both spoke Yiddish as well as French. Part of the fun Henriette and I had was teaching Suzanne some rather unkind phrases in Yiddish that she didn't mind using from time to time. Hearing her speak Yiddish with her southern French accent made both Henriette and me burst into laughter every time, especially when she was telling someone to kiss her touress! Thinking back on the risks we took, I am amazed that Henriette and I were never detained as Jews and sent to concentration camps, along with Suzanne for aiding us. Jacqueline, on the other hand, was the quiet, reserved one of the bunch. Although she was younger than the three of us, she was very serious, never clowning around or joking as we three did. She was also dating a young man named Pierre and seemed just as in love with him as Henriette was in love with Bernard, a handsome young man she had met in Paris and encountered again once she had gotten to Marseilles. Suzanne was also involved with a young man, Antoine Rabbia, whom she had met while visiting her sister who lived in Nice. However, Antoine was in the military and stationed in Turkey, so while Henriette and Jacqueline spent the weekends with their boyfriends, Suzanne and I spent time together trying to find ways to entertain ourselves. Someone had a phonograph and records that we would listen to from time to time. Being young and sometimes insensitive, we would sit in the window looking out at the people walking by and making fun of them while we laughed about their idiosyncrasies.

Although life took on a semblance of a routine, there always seemed to be some kind of drama going on, especially with Henriette. Every morning we would get up and get ready to go to prayers and breakfast followed by each of us going our separate ways to work. Since Henriette worked as a tailor, she would just stay at the home to complete her work in a room they had designated for her sewing machine. Jacqueline worked as a secretary on the other side of town from where Suzanne and I worked. Although the water warehouse was farther away than the photography studio where Suzanne worked, we would walk to work together until we got to the studio where I would leave her and go on to my job. At lunchtime, I would walk back to the photography studio where Suzanne would join me for the remainder of the walk back to the home. We would have lunch together with the other girls and then head back to our prospective jobs until

BRENDA HANCOCK

the end of the workday. In the evenings Suzanne would wait for me at the photography studio, and we would walk together back to the home for our dinner.

One day shortly after I had arrived at the photography studio to pick up Suzanne for lunch, a girl from the home came running up to us, breathlessly telling us that we needed to hurry back to the home for some crisis with Henriette. As we rushed back, she filled us in on as much as she knew. The door to our room had been left open, and Henriette was inside, lying on the bed and crying out for Suzanne and me. As we raced up the stairs to our room, we had no idea what to expect. There lay Henriette, loudly sobbing and vowing between sobs that she was dying. Before rushing out to fetch a doctor, we gathered from her that she had taken a bottle of aspirin in desperation. It seems that Bernard had broken up with her, and her immediate reaction was that she did not want to live any longer if she had to live without him! We both declared that she was crazy to do this over a boy as we raced to find a doctor who would come at lunchtime. This could prove to be quite difficult since everyone knew that lunch was at least a two-hour affair for the French. Fortunately, we found someone fairly quickly and practically dragged him back to the home to help our friend survive. He pumped her stomach and assured us that the bottle of aspirin had done no permanent harm. We had barely relaxed from our fears of losing Henriette when we were unceremoniously summoned downstairs. Madame Perdeno was furious with us all and explained the severity of our actions. Too late, we learned that there was a doctor affiliated with the home who was supposed to take care of any problems. Our calling in another doctor was severe enough to warrant our being kicked out of the home. Before the fear of being evicted could sink in, Madame Perdeno smiled at us, called us crazy, and sent us on our way, warning us never again to cause such a commotion or we REALLY would be kicked out.

Hurrying back to work, Suzanne and I could not believe how much trouble Henriette had caused, all over some stupid boy! We had missed our lunch while sitting on the steps outside the room waiting for the doctor and Madame Perdeno to come out to let us know if Henriette would survive. We had almost gotten kicked out of the home. To make matters worse, we both were late getting back to work and would have a lot of explaining to do to our bosses just to keep our jobs!

Another time Suzanne and I almost got kicked out of the home was Suzanne's fault. She had gotten a letter from Antoine saying he would be on leave in a small town near Marseilles and for her to come meet him for the weekend. Of course, a young, unmarried girl could not appear to go off for the weekend to visit a boyfriend, so Suzanne wrote down that she was spending the weekend with her boss and his family. Unfortunately, she did not make it home before time to go to work on Monday. Her boss called the nuns to see why she hadn't come in to work, blowing her cover for the weekend away. When I came in at lunch, Madame Perdeno called me in and said I had to go see the nuns across the street. I had hardly gotten in the room when they asked me where Suzanne was. I told them that she was with her boss, to which they replied, "You are LYING!" Unknown to me, Suzanne had come in earlier and eventually told them she had gone to see her fiancé and his family instead of her boss and his family. As I sat there being accused of lying and not knowing what to say, Suzanne came into the room and said, "They know. I told them." As far as the nuns were concerned, we should both be kicked out for lying. Once again, Madame Perdeno came to our rescue and convinced the nuns that we needed to stay there and would be good from then on.

Madame Perdeno was extremely helpful and kind to me. I had gotten word from Madeleine that she had married Jean Wegier and that she was with her mother-in-law and sister-in-law and some other family somewhere in the country not far away. They had heard that the Germans were getting closer and that they would need to leave or be in big trouble, risking capture and deportation. Worried that she had no other alternative, Madeleine wrote to me and asked if she could come and stay with me at the home for girls. Already having been saved from being kicked out in the streets more than once by Madame Perdeno, I went to her to ask her help. We had spent many hours visiting with Madame Perdeno and had learned that she hated the Germans because her son had died at their hands. Deciding the only thing that would work was to tell her the truth, I not only let her know that I was Jewish and that I needed help to save my sister, but I also told her about my being a courier for the Underground in the hopes that she would appreciate the things I was doing to fight the Germans and help my sister out. Telling me how very brave she thought I was, she told me that Madeleine could come to stay with me. As it turned out, Madeleine never came. She had found a job as a nanny in Lyon and was safe for the time being, but she thanked me for the help. After that, I did not hear from her again until after the war when I returned to Paris.

Another crazy thing that Suzanne, Henriette, and I would do happened when the sirens would go off in the evening to warn the people of Marseilles about potential bombings. The siren was to indicate that everyone should go to designated bomb shelters throughout the city. French guards, wearing helmets, gas masks, and whistles, would herd the people into the various shelters throughout the town once the sirens went off. Instead of heading downstairs to the shelter when we heard the sirens, we would go up to the top floor where we would go out on the balcony and wave at the planes as they flew over. Fortunately for us, the bombs were not dropped anywhere near us. Although she didn't know of this risk we took, it's no wonder Madame Perdeno called us crazy. At any moment those planes could have dropped their bombs right on top of us, but we were young and did not think of the risk involved. We were just thrilled to know the Americans were nearby.

CHAPTER 10

Change of Plans

This existence I had created for myself in Marseilles was something I thought would go on indefinitely, probably until the end of the war. With Suzanne, Henriette, and Jacqueline becoming my surrogate family, I was comfortable, even living among the Germans who were constantly there to remind us that it was actually wartime in France. I went to a job that I enjoyed and was praised for doing a good job. I completed missions with the Underground and received great satisfaction every time I learned that I had been instrumental in any kind of defeat of the Germans. I laughed and joked as young people do with my three friends. Never did I guess that this existence would come to an abrupt end.

Since it was nearing lunchtime, I was headed to pick up Suzanne as usual on a warm, sunny day in May of 1944 when the sirens went off and suddenly the streets were filled with people. The guards with their helmets, whistles, and gas masks ordered people to go to the nearest shelter as quickly as possible while French and Germans alike were scurrying through the streets. I went into the nearest shelter, located at the train station. Being young, I guess I just didn't have the patience that I should have had. After staying below for what seemed like far too long for me (but which was probably only ten minutes or so), I left the shelter and headed in search of Suzanne. I hadn't gone many blocks before I was herded into a second shelter and the bombs began raining down on the town of Marseilles. These bombs were being dropped by the Americans, and we'd often teased that the English managed to always hit their targets, but American bombs hit everything. That particular day in Marseilles, the Americans seemed to be living up to this notion, for it seemed they were hitting everything. The bombing seemed to go on forever, and I don't believe I have ever done as much praying in my life as I did in that shelter as the bombs kept pouring down on the city.

Finally, the siren went off to indicate the peril was over, and we emerged from the shelter to see if there was anything left of the city. From the noise and the trembling of the earth in the shelter, we were sure we'd come out of the shelter to find the whole city had been leveled. Fortunately, that was not quite the case; however, the damage was quite extensive. As I gingerly picked my way down the streets trying to hurry back to the home to see if everyone was OK, I found myself passing the most unbelievable sight I had seen to that point. There were dead bodies everywhere, as well as wounded people lying bloody on the ground being helped by still others who may or may not have been wounded themselves. Pieces of buildings were scattered everywhere. The more carnage I saw the greater my fear that my beloved friends would not have survived. Instead of stopping to try to help, my feet raced along the streets jumping over debris and carrying me past the dead bodies, not letting me stop until I made it back to the home.

When I finally made my way back to the home, it seemed as if a miracle had taken place. The buildings had not been hit at all and looked exactly as they had that morning when I left for work.

BRENDA HANCOCK

I raced inside to find my three friends all waiting there for me, just as glad to see me alive and unhurt as I was to see them. We raced into each others' arms and kissed and hugged as we each shared our experiences during the bombing—where we had been and what it had sounded like to us. Each story showed that we all had felt as if the world were coming to an end with the incessant noise and shaking of the earth that accompanied all of the bombs. We discovered that of all the girls in the home, only one had been injured, and her injuries were so slight that she'd been released from the hospital that afternoon. Sadly for many others, though, we also learned that around three thousand people died that day in Marseilles. Perhaps the most frightening thing to me was my learning that many of the dead were people who had gone into the first shelter where I had only waited about ten minutes before leaving. Had I stayed there, I probably would not have made it out alive that day since one of the bombs had made a direct hit on that shelter. Once again, for some reason unknown to me, I was one of the lucky ones who escaped without a scratch.

Within a couple of days of the bombing, I got a call to meet with Monsieur Phillippe. I was surprised when they gave me no message or ammunition to carry. When I got there, Phillippe had instructions for me instead. I'm not sure if it was because of the bombings or because of something urgent elsewhere, but Phillippe told me that I was being given orders to leave Marseilles and go to Agen, located about four hundred kilometers to the west in the Lot et Garonne departement of France where I would continue to carry out missions. I needed to be ready to go as soon as possible. As I rode the bicycle back to Marseilles, I wondered about this move. I'd have to leave behind the comfort of my friends, the job that gave me security, everything I had come to know. Before I could become frightened and talk myself out of it, I reminded myself that I'd left people much closer to me with nothing before and had made it just fine. I could do this, too.

When I returned to the home, I went straight to Madame Perdeno's office to let her know that I would be leaving. Since she knew I was in the Underground, I gave her the real reason for my going, telling her that I'd been "transferred" to Agen. She said she was sorry to see me go and wished me good luck and good fortune as she hugged me before letting me leave her office. Just about the time I left her office, it was time for dinner, so I met up with Suzanne, Henriette, and Jacqueline and talked about everyday things as we ate our dinner. Once we were back in our room, I broke the news to my friends. No sooner had the words left my mouth than Suzanne said, "I'm coming with you. Agen isn't too far from Montauban, and you don't need to go alone. I'm coming, too."

Before I could answer her, Henriette piped in that she, too, would come with me to Agen. Since she basically worked for herself, she felt she could find work wherever she might go and didn't want to be left without Suzanne and me. Jacqueline was the only one who decided to remain there. She had a good job and her boyfriend and didn't want to leave either. Her decision seemed to make more sense than that of Suzanne and Henriette—just picking up and leaving because I was leaving—but I was truly glad to know that they would come with me and that I would not be alone in a city where I knew no one.

Monsieur Pianelli was just as kind as Madame Perdeno had been when I told him I could no longer work for him because I was leaving Marseilles. Perhaps it was because of the massive bombings that had just occurred, but no one questioned my leaving, and Madame Perdeno was the only one who knew the real reason for my departure. Monsieur Pianelli, too, wished me well in my journeys as well as in life as he hugged me good-bye that last day.

Within three days of my getting the message of my "transfer" to Agen, Suzanne, Henriette, and I were on a train carrying our meager possessions along for this new adventure. Arriving in Agen, we decided to try the Catholic Home located there for possible lodging. Our room in Marseilles had not been the largest or most beautifully decorated room in the town, but it was quite comfortable for us. If there were similar arrangements in Agen, we would be glad to move into them. Much to our dismay, the home in Agen was not like the home in Marseilles. Instead of the three of us being able to share our own room and have some privacy, we ended up in a large dormitory room with other girls of all ages, including many who were quite young. We could only take a week of living with the small children before we decided we had to find other arrangements.

During the week we lived in the dormitory at the home that turned out to be an orphanage, we accomplished several other things—or perhaps I should say that we settled several things. Within two days of our arrival, I managed to come up with a lame excuse for Suzanne and Henriette that would give me the time to make contact with the member of the Underground I was instructed to find. My contact was to be a Commandant Francois—I learned that this was not his real name and although I was with him until the boys were ordered to go on into Germany and the women were told to go home, I never knew any other name for him. Upon making contact, I discovered that my "job" there would be similar to what I'd been doing in Marseilles—at least, that's what it started out being.

As for work, Henriette was lucky and found work in a dress shop very soon after we arrived in Agen. Once again it wasn't what I knew but who I knew that got me the "civilian" job that would pay the bills. Suzanne had a cousin who lived not far away from the orphanage. Two good things came as a result of this cousin—first was that she knew about a job in a food warehouse whose duties sounded to be much like what I'd done in Marseilles. With her help, I got this job. Second, when we could stand the dormitory with its lack of privacy no longer, the cousin let us come and stay with her for a few days. Suzanne looked for work for a whole week, but then decided it would be best for her to simply return to Montauban rather than be a burden to her cousin or to us when we found other accommodations. Within a couple of days, Henriette and I found a room we could rent in a house owned by two old ladies and settled into our routine of going to work and coming back to share our space much as we had in Marseilles. Also like in Marseilles, I would be contacted to go on a mission to deliver messages or guns or ammunition. Amazingly, Henriette never questioned the lame excuses I would give her for being gone.

CHAPTER 11

The Horror and Then They Are Gone

My duties as courier in the Marseilles area had just about become routine. I would pack my satchel carefully, hoping the Germans would look no further than the books on top or question its heaviness when I carried guns or ammunition. I would travel by bus or by bicycle to the appointed meeting, always being stopped by the Germans, who asked my destination and purpose in traveling. Upon arrival, I would pass along whatever I had taken with me and then return home, often being stopped again by Germans wanting to know my destination and reason for traveling. Despite my many missions, I had not seen any blood or violence until the bombing of Marseilles. All of that changed during my job as a courier in Agen. Whether it was just that I had not witnessed it before or that it had not happened before and was an indication of the desperation of the Germans, I was not sure, but the things I saw in my travels as courier for the Underground based in Agen burned in my memory, increasing my hatred for the Germans in a way I thought it would be impossible for it to do. After all, I had been thrust from my home, had my family taken away from me, and had lost the innocent life I had known as a result of the Germans. How could my hatred for them grow?

That question was first answered one day as I was traveling on a mission. I had to pass through several small villages before I reached my destination and was cycling along not thinking of anything in particular except my determination to successfully complete the mission. My thoughts immediately changed as I neared a small village and heard a cacophony of harsh shouts and heart-wrenching cries unlike any I had heard before. As I pulled into the town, my shock and horror at what I saw was intensified by the sight of angry German soldiers herding everyone into the square in front of the church. I, too, was pushed along by the barrel of a German rifle and harsh words that could only mean something like, "Hurry! Gather together!" As I stood there holding onto my bicycle and looking around to see what all the commotion was about, my grip on the bicycle became so intense that I could easily have choked the Germans holding the guns on me and my fellow Frenchmen. I could hardly believe what I was seeing as the tears began to stream down my face.

A young man was holding onto a young lady, and they both were screaming and crying in a way that seemed incomprehensible until I looked at the church door. Standing near the door and pointing to it was an arrogant, angry German officer who was shouting and pointing at the door itself. When my eyes finally focused on the door, shock stirred emotions in me that I never knew could exist. A beautiful baby was hanging on the door with its arms outstretched and nails going through its hands and feet—it had been crucified just like Jesus, only it was these monsters, these Germans who had taken the baby from its parents' arms and nailed it to the church to teach the town a lesson. We, the townspeople and anyone who happened to be traveling through, had to stand there at gunpoint and watch the helpless parents see their innocent baby die in retaliation for the death of a German soldier

BRENDA HANCOCK

during the night. From the ravings of that mad German, I could tell that he was letting the French know exactly what happens when one of us kills one of them. It all seemed so senseless. I could understand a soldier killing another soldier—after all, that's what war was all about. I could understand a soldier killing someone like me, a person in the Underground fighting against them. I could NOT understand the killing of an innocent baby. That baby had nothing to do with the murder of the German soldier, and from what I could tell, his parents had nothing to do with it either. The German officer had just decided to teach us all a lesson, to show how little our lives meant to them and that we were ALL his enemy, even the innocent children. After twenty to thirty minutes of listening to his speech about what happens to anyone who dares to kill a German, the officer decided the show was over and we could go. Tears still streamed down my face as I pedaled away from that village, and I knew that the hatred I had felt previously toward the Germans was nothing compared to what it was at that moment.

My destination was not far enough away to erase those terrible memories from my mind, so I was still crying when I reached my contact. Showing great concern, he asked me what was wrong, what had happened to cause such distress. Through my sobs, I managed to tell him what I had just witnessed. Although he tried to comfort me, to help quiet my tears, he also told me that what I had seen was not unusual. I realized how much I had been shielded from the actuality of this war as he told me about one of the commanders of the Underground and what he had to witness. It seems the son of the commander was also in the Underground and had been caught. In order to try to get him to give out information, they had burned out his eyes and pulled off all his fingernails in front of the townspeople, including his father, before finally killing him because he refused to give any information.

In another instance, he had heard of three members of the Underground who had been caught and were to be hung. Again, in front of the entire village, the Germans had the men lined up ready to be hung. Before putting the rope on one of the men, the German in charge of putting the rope around their necks was shocked by the Frenchman who spit in his face to show how little respect he had for this enemy who was not worthy of even being his executioner. Then the Frenchman looked the German squarely in the eye and said, "Give me the rope and I'll do it myself. I don't want you to touch me!"

The worst he had heard was of an eleven-year-old boy whose cousin had killed some Germans. This cousin had been wounded, so the Germans thought he went to his uncle, the boy's father, for help. In reality, he had not come to his uncle at all, but the Germans still took the man and his fourteen-year-old son for harboring an enemy and killed them both along with several other townspeople. The eleven-year-old was then dragged from his house to a place where the dead were piled up so that he could identify his father and brother and take the bodies away for burial. Hearing these stories and others along the way only made my resolve to defeat this enemy get stronger and stronger. I was willing to do anything to remove them from my life and my country.

Getting rid of the Germans turned out to be much simpler than I ever imagined. One night in August of 1944, Henriette and I prepared to go to bed but found sleep hard to come by since there was such a commotion in the streets below us. Knowing how the Germans might react, we were afraid to look out to see what was going on, but speculated on the noise well into the night before sleep ever came. The next morning when we went down to breakfast, we asked our landlady if she knew what all the noise was about. To our amazement she simply said, "The Germans left." It was such a simple statement, but it reminded me of my father's having said, "One night you will go to bed with the

Germans and wake up the next morning to find them gone." Sure enough, once we went out into the streets, we saw the truth of her words—not one single German could be seen anywhere, no German trucks, no other German vehicles of any kind, nothing but Frenchmen who were just as elated as we were to have them gone. Thrilled at having them gone, I didn't go to work that day, but went straight to my commander to see what would be next for me.

Upon my arrival, I saw not only my commander, but several men all preparing to go off to fight. Although I wasn't sure exactly how he would react to my request, I blurted out that I wanted to go with them and fight, too. At first he didn't say anything, and I was prepared to give him every argument I could think of to let me go along. To my surprise, he agreed without my having to press my case, but I'm sure I would have pestered him and done everything in my power to go along if he'd said that I couldn't go just because I was a girl. I was so excited I could have kissed him, but restrained myself and just said I would go make preparations and be ready to leave whenever he told me. He assured me as I almost ran away from him in my excitement that I had at least two days before they would leave.

First, I went to my job and told my boss that since the Germans were gone, I would try to go back home. It wasn't quite the truth, but it was close enough and just like my boss in Marseilles, he wished me well. Then I went straight to Henriette to let her know that I'd be leaving. We had already been through so much, and I didn't want to leave her without a proper explanation since I was sure my leaving would also change her circumstances and life. For the first time, I told her what I'd been doing in Marseilles as well as in Agen and explained that the Underground was heading out to liberate other towns in France and I was going with them. It was my plan to try to go all the way to Germany to try to find my family. Although she was a bit shocked that all this time she thought I was just some silly young French girl like her and instead I had been secretly fighting the Germans, she was also very proud of me and understood my need to try to find my family. After deciding that she would also leave Agen and join her parents in the south of France, she went with me to tell our landlady. As we packed our meager belongings, we agreed that we would not lose touch with each other and would meet again in Paris after the war was finally over.

CHAPTER 12

On the Road with the FFI

On the second day after the Germans had left Agen I reported to my commander with my few belongings packed in my satchel that had served me so well since leaving Paris. He took me to a school where the men were gathering, and we stayed there for a few more days before leaving Agen, sleeping on the floor or wherever we could get comfortable. The citizens of Agen rounded up what we called Milice or blackshirts, Frenchmen and women who had collaborated with the Germans. They were lined up in the town square with the town gathered around to see what would be done. Apparently, the Frenchmen felt that the Milice were worse than the Germans, and they shouted, "Kill them!" The men in the Underground were just as unhappy with the Milice as the townspeople and would gladly have killed them, but the commander did not want to lower himself to the level of the Germans, who too frequently lined people up in the town square for public execution. Consequently, all the Milice were put in prison instead; however, the commander didn't see anything wrong with letting them feel a little fear and did not stop his men from pretending they were going to execute them. They would line them up and begin counting as if they would all fire at the same time. Finally, the commander decided these blackshirts had endured enough for one day, declared that they needed to be judged properly, and had the men escort them all to prison to await their trials.

Each night the members of the Underground would try to get comfortable enough to sleep on the floors of the school. Although I was the only girl there, they all treated me with the greatest respect and never made any lewd advances. At first, I was sure I was being protected by the commander, who would never let them think of me as anything less than their equal. As we traveled along and encountered other groups of Underground, it became clear that the men of my group thought of me as their sister. Any time any of the other fighters decided their celebrations at removing Germans should include a tryst with me, my guys would immediately make it clear that I was off-limits.

Only one member of our group was Jewish, and he never blew my cover with the other guys. His cousin had lived in our apartment building, and although we had never visited before, he seemed to recognize me. He came up to me and said that I looked very familiar. When I told him I had lived on Rue des Deux Ponts in Paris, he remembered having seen me from time to time during his visits to his cousin. However, after establishing where he'd seen me before, we never openly discussed our being Jewish with the others and really didn't even spend any extra time together. I had left Cecile behind and was now Nick, the Catholic girl, to everyone, which was fine with him. I don't even know if the others knew he was Jewish—it just wasn't something either of us wanted known.

After a couple of days in Agen, we went to Fazanis, where we stayed for two or three weeks preparing to go forth and liberate the towns. Although we were anxious to head on out, it took a while to gather the trucks, supplies, and a cannon to use along the way and to get everything else organized with the other groups of Underground also preparing to go out and liberate France. In addition to the supplies, we were all given armbands that had the Cross of Lorraine on them. This signified that we were with the FFI, Forces Françaises de l'Intérieur, directly under the leadership of Charles de Gaulle, whose home town was in Lorraine. While there, we again found accommodations wherever we could, sometimes sleeping in trucks or busses, sometimes on the floor of a school or church. During this time I began to form friendships and assured the men in my group that I had every intention of holding up my end in the fight for liberating these towns. Before long, most of them knew I intended to go all the way to Germany to try to find my family.

When we finally were all set to leave, the anticipation and the waiting had built up such energy in us all that I'm certain we could have defeated a battalion of Germans. As it turned out, the Germans had left most of the towns by the time we got there, just as they had evacuated Agen—without one gun ever being fired.

Me with some of my unit traveling through southern France liberating towns.

Only rarely did my group ever have to do any fighting. In one small town, a couple of Germans were captured. My group brought them to me to guard while they scoured the rest of the town to make sure it was secure. As I held the gun on them, I thought this would be my perfect opportunity to get the revenge I'd been wanting for years. The Germans had taken my family, and I was fairly certain that I would never see my parents again since they were old. Stories of what happened once the Jews arrived in Germany had leaked across the border, and I'd seen for myself how ruthless the Germans could be. None of the stories I'd heard or the things I'd seen gave me any hope that my parents would still be alive—maybe my little brother and surely my strong-willed sister, but not them and not my small nephews who'd been taken with my parents.

My eyes must have given away my thoughts because I saw the fear in their eyes. They knew I had no qualms about taking their lives. However, as I looked at them, I realized that killing these two Germans would not bring my family back to me. Killing them with no justifiable reason other than that they were Germans would only make me as heartless and cruel as the Germans had been to us. I might have lost my youthful innocence and my family, but I didn't want to lose my. decency as a human being. I didn't want to become the animal that I'd seen in them, randomly killing anyone wearing a German uniform as they'd randomly killed Frenchmen just because they were French. Finally, I told the Germans that if they gave me any excuse, I would gladly blow them away, but if they remained still and didn't try anything, they would live. I was speaking French, but they either understood the language or understood my tone because they didn't budge the whole time I guarded them.

Most of those travels from Agen north heading toward Paris and Germany ended up being celebrations instead of battles. We would enter a village or small town to find that the Germans were

BRENDA HANCOCK

Me as Pierrette Nicodem with the men of my unit on our way to liberate small towns in southern France.

already gone and that the townspeople were thrilled to see us. They would give us wine, bread, and food to celebrate their freedom with us. At night we would look for some place to sleep, often having to make do with the floors of a school or church again. In one particular town, the men had no choice but to sleep on the bus we were using to travel. Some were on the seats, while still others were on the floor. I left in search of a room, but after checking everywhere and having no luck, I returned to the bus to find most of the guys already asleep. One of my friends saw me return and offered his seat, moving to the floor of the bus. One of his buddies sleeping on the floor below my seat didn't know I'd taken the spot. Sleeping with my backside facing outward, I was suddenly awakened early the next morning by a slap on my behind and garbled words to the effect that it was time to get my lazy butt up and be ready for another day of saving France. Obviously, seeing me instead of his buddy on the seat was a great shock to my friend in combat. His embarrassment was only intensified by the teasing of the rest of the guys who'd awakened in time to witness his slapping of my butt instead of his buddy's. Mortified by what he'd done, he kept apologizing for the rest of the day, despite my trying to assure him that no harm had been done.

Not only did these men in my group of the Underground earn a permanent place in my heart, but also along the way I met a few fighters from other groups who etched their own places in my heart as well. One such person was Hughes Beau, a fighter with one of the Communist factions of the Underground whom I met in Sancergues. Upon our arrival in town, I went to the store to see if they knew of any rooms available in the town. The shopkeeper told me that to his knowledge, all the rooms in the town were taken. Thinking I would have to spend yet another night on a floor or a seat of the bus, I turned to go, but was stopped by a young man who was obviously with the Underground, too, but in a different branch. Explaining that he had a room for the night, but that he was scheduled for guard duty and wouldn't be using it, he offered me the key to his room. Before he left, he made me promise to lock the door once I got in and not to open it except when I heard a special knock that would indicate he was returning. When I questioned this, he explained that the group he was with were not to be trusted with a young lady—that they'd had too much to drink and had not been around women for a while. I assured him that I was not afraid, that I had a gun and wasn't afraid to use it, but he insisted that I promise to follow his instructions about the door before he would let me have the key. For that night, I had a very comfortable bed and a solid night's sleep. The next morning, this generous young man returned, gave the spe-

BRENDA HANCOCK

cial knock, and invited me to breakfast. Throughout that morning we visited and I learned about his privileged childhood that included nannies, about the wonderful girl he'd fallen in love with and married, about his beautiful son, and about why he was working with the Communists. It turned out that the only group forming where he lived happened to be Communist, so he joined them just to be able to fight against the Germans.

When he asked me what I was doing there, I explained that I was fighting with the FFI. Although he saw my armband with the Cross of Lorraine, it shocked him to think of a woman risking her life, but I explained that since my family was all gone, I just didn't care about my life any more. Just then he didn't have much to say about this, but it must have made an impact on him. For several days we stayed in that town, but I rejoined my group and slept on the floor at the school, this time protected against the drunken revelers by my friends who would never let their "sister" be molested. I guess I was a bit of an oddity, though, because in all our travels and all our encounters with other resistance groups, I was the only girl.

After being in Sancergues for several days, our commander finally got orders, ones that would crush my hopes of going to Germany to find my family. In essence, the orders said that all male members of the Underground were officially in the army now. They even got uniforms and were "real" soldiers who were scheduled to fight their way to Germany. All women in the Underground were told to go home, that their service was now ended. No matter how much I begged, orders were orders, and I was forbidden to go any further. Before I left, I was given two parties to say good-bye. On the last day, my members of the FFI gave me a dinner at which they presented me with a notebook in which they had each put a picture and signed with a note so that I would never forget them. In addition the officers gave me the money to go home. I hated to see them go, not only because I wanted to be with them, but also because I had become very close to them all. They were my guys.

On that same day, I was given a going-away party by Hughes Beau and some of his friends. He, too, gave me his picture and wrote some words that made me realize how seriously he'd taken my statement that my life meant nothing to me. Although I later learned that he'd been killed, his words remain with me, amazing me at how true they were, even though I doubted seriously that what he had to say could ever be true. He wrote, "Life is a marvelous thing because it always brings the future. At your age all your life is going to open up for you, and soon someone will take a big place in your heart. And then there will be little ones, and that will be the most beautiful in the world. In life there will always be hard times, but they will have their consolations. Know

Hughes Beau's words of wisdom to me about my future with my own children.

BRENDA HANCOCK

that happiness will come to you and will stay with you—That's what I wish for you."

Sadly, I watched the men with whom I'd formed such a bond go off toward Germany without me. Since my job with the Underground was over and there was nothing for me to do in Sancergues, I took the train back to Paris, hoping to find one of my aunts or anyone in my family still alive.

CHAPTER 13

Back in Paris with the CAVF

By the time the train arrived in Paris, it was already evening in early October, 1944. Not having any idea if I would find anyone in my family still alive, I thought the best thing would be to go to the apartment of my aunt Sara Esther, my father's younger sister, who had also emigrated from Poland to Paris. I picked her because her apartment had been closest to the train station where I arrived, hoping that if she were not there, perhaps one of her neighbors might know where she or her family could be found.

When I knocked at the door, I awaited its opening with great uncertainty, not knowing for sure where I would go if she no longer lived there. Imagine my joy and hers as well when she opened the door! Much to my surprise, she told me that she had never left her apartment and basically had come through the war and the German occupation much better than my immediate family. Of her seven children, only her husband and two of her older married daughters had been taken. Her oldest son was also a prisoner of war, not in a concentration camp, at the time. Her four teenage children were there at home with her and welcomed me to their dinner table, giving me a place to stay for the night.

She also had good news to tell me. My brother Jacques and my sister Fanny were both still in Paris and had never been "bothered" either.

Shortly after breakfast the next morning, I left my aunt and cousins and went to see Jacques. When my sister-in-law Gaby answered the door, she looked as if she were seeing a ghost since they had not heard from me or seen me for over two years. Much to my amazement, our joy, kisses, and happiness were barely expressed when my sister-in-law told me, "If you plan to stay here, you must know that I am NOT your mother. You will do what I tell you to do if you live here!" At the age of twenty-one after having survived on my own for over two years, I didn't think I could live under the thumb of my bossy sister-in-law. I politely told her thank you very much and left shortly after those welcoming words from her.

Still not knowing for sure where I might stay or what I might do, I took a chance by going back to the Pletzl of Paris near where I had grown up, walking the streets looking for anyone I might know. After a while, I met an old schoolmate named Olga, who had not only gone to school with me, but had also spent summers in Colleville. She still lived near the school and said that she and her family weren't "bothered" during the occupation because her twin brothers had been in the army. One had died fighting in the war, and the other was a prisoner of war. Then she asked me what I'd been doing, where I'd been. After I explained my escape from Paris and my ending up working in the Underground, she told me that she'd read in the paper that any girl who had documented proof of service in the Underground could serve in a new organization called the CAVF or Corps Auxilliaire Voluntaire Feminin. I followed her back to her apartment to get the paper and the address, once again realizing how luck was still with me.

Since it was still early in the day, I went to the address listed in the newspaper, where I was sent to Capitaine Nicole

Brunswick, who signed me up immediately upon viewing my letter from Commandant Francois, which proved my service. She took me to my room at the Hotel de la Tremoille, a single room that, even though small, was very nice. Next, she took me to the tailor who made uniforms for all the girls in the CAVF. While waiting for mine to be made, she gave me a used uniform to wear. Next, she told me that the CAVF was divided into five different areas of service to see which one would fit me best. The five areas consisted of social service worker, translator, secretary, driver, or telephone operator. She decided that I would best fit as a social service worker. In this capacity, it would be my job to go to the hospital to visit those who had been wounded until the war was actually over.

My first assignment was to visit a young man who had been captured and tried to escape by jumping six floors down to the pavement while in custody at the police station. It seems that he had decided they would kill him anyway, so he felt the risk was worth the attempt. The fall had broken his back, and he was paralyzed from the neck down. Since we had uniforms, we could go and come in the hospitals as we wished, not having to adhere to visiting hours. It was our job to visit, try to cheer, write to family, or help in other nonmedical services. The first time I went, another member of the CAVF accompanied me, and I continued to visit with that first young man until he seemed to be getting a bit serious. I was able to find someone else to take his case. Part of the job included visiting women who had children to see if they needed any help. After each visit, we had to report the condition of the people we had visited to a doctor, who would then go take care of anyone in need of medical services.

Not only did my service in the CAVF provide me with my room, but I also was given three meals a day at the hotel along with a small salary. Although I never had to share a room, there were some larger rooms at the hotel that two girls had to share.

Me with CAVF friends Solange and Ramonde.

During this early time of my service, I made two very good friends, Solange and Raymonde. Solange was a nurse who worked with the doctor who provided medical services. Raymonde served in the secretarial division. The hotel had a large lobby where we would gather in the evenings after dinner to visit. Our uniforms not only gave us extra privileges at the hospitals, but they also enabled us to go into any American club or theater. Often in the evenings, Solange, Raymonde, and I would go to the clubs to dance or to the theater to see a production. We must have made an interesting combination since Raymonde was very tall, Solange was of medium height, and I was very short. It was here that my love for dancing and American music grew. Again, the talent in my family was not all taken by my siblings. Once the GIs saw me dance one dance, I had a constant stream of partners every night for as long as the three of us stayed at the club. At the club, there were Americans, English, Canadians, and a few Frenchmen, and I danced with them all.

Just as the war ended, the government requisitioned the Hotel

Lutecia to be used for incoming political prisoners returning from concentration camps in Germany. My first job required me to go to Orly Field to receive incoming prisoners. Along with two other girls, I processed the prisoners, getting their names and addresses so we could notify their families and checking the severity of their injuries to make sure they got proper medical care. Because many of these prisoners were very ill, we were required to have typhus shots. We were supposed to have a series of three shots, but I only had one. Just before I was scheduled for my second shot, a new group of prisoners had arrived. As usual, I asked if anyone had seen any of my family. One man said he'd seen my brother and my father, which greatly surprised me since my father was so old. I asked for a description and soon realized he was talking about my brother-in-law Jacques, Ida's husband. Although the news was good, he only remembered having seen them, but couldn't remember exactly when or what might have happened to them since. After hearing that, I just could not receive the shot. Try as he might, the doctor could not get the needle to pierce the skin in my back. He told me I would have to come back, but I never went back for the second shot or the third. I just didn't have the time.

Luck was still with me despite my not having the full series of shots. One day shortly after the failed second attempt at a shot, a plane arrived with a new group of returning prisoners. As usual, we would greet the prisoners with hugs and kisses to welcome them back to French soil. One of the young men coming down from the plane looked especially ill. His whole face and head were covered with open, oozing sores that would repulse even the strongest at heart. Despite his condition, I reached to welcome him back with the customary kisses on both cheeks, much to his surprise. As I stretched up to give him his welcoming kisses, he asked me if I weren't afraid of catching what he obviously had. He was sure no one would want to touch him, but I told him that

I wasn't afraid and he deserved the same welcome home as any Frenchman. I cried as I reached up to gently kiss both his cheeks, not wanting to cause him any more pain. After the welcome, I assured him there would be plenty of people to take care of him and that all would soon be well. Unfortunately, since we saw so many each day, there was little or no way to make sure that I'd told him the truth and that he would indeed be totally well one day. Although I didn't really care at that point whether I got sick or not, I never developed any symptoms after kissing that poor boy.

The very next day I was back at Orly for the arrival of another plane of prisoners. Although the pilot was a tall, extremely good-looking young man who caught my eye, he didn't talk to any of us girls, and the arrival of the prisoners took my attention away from him. First off the plane was a French general, and it was my duty to greet him and take his information. As I kissed him, again I cried. He asked me why I was crying, and I replied, "You look exactly like my father, and I'm pretty sure he has not survived." This slender man with a goatee looked so much like my father that it brought back all the pain of the loss I had tried for almost three years to push to the back of my mind. If I just didn't think about it, it wouldn't hurt so much to be alone. Yet, here stood a man that was almost the image of my father, causing the loss to come rushing back at me like a tidal wave. He put his arm around me and patted my shoulder, saying that my father would come back, too. My response was that from all I'd heard the fact that he was a Jew made the chances of his coming back just about impossible. Despite my words, he told me not to lose hope.

Pulling myself together, I got down to the business at hand—this great general had to be processed. His name was General Audibert, and originally from Bretagne, he had been in charge of four large areas of the Underground before being captured. First, I sent a telegram to his family to let them know he had arrived at

Orly and would be home soon. In addition, he needed to be cleared by a doctor and to have his official papers done. Before I left him in the care of the doctor, he asked me for my name and address. Two weeks later much to my surprise, I received a card from him, thanking me for the help I'd given him on his return from Buchenwald. I kept it along with the memory of his encouraging words, amazed that so important a general could be that kind and thoughtful to an unimportant individual like myself.

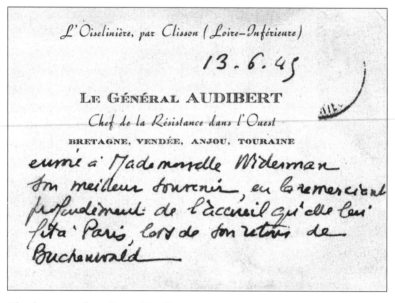

Thank you note from General Audibert.

BRENDA HANCOCK

CHAPTER 14

Finding My Brother Alive

By May of 1945 the war was over and a huge influx of prisoners was being sent back to Paris for repatriation. To accommodate the great numbers that needed to be processed, three separate shifts were created so that we could work around the clock. The first shift was from 7 A.M. until around 4 P.M., with the second shift covering 4 P.M. until midnight, and the third shift lasting from midnight until 7 A.M. If we worked the midnight until 7 shift, we would not have to work again until 7 the following morning. After work on the first shift, we would leave the Hotel Lutecia and go to a nearby club run by the American Red Cross and available for anyone wearing a military uniform. Since we were in uniforms as well, we were welcomed there. When we worked the night shift and got off at midnight, we would go straight back to our hotel to sleep, but after the third shift, we sometimes stayed awake until afternoon when we could go to the club. Although they served coffee and donuts (something we had never seen or tasted before), the main draw for us was the music. Instead of listening to records, there we saw and heard the performances live.

The greatest thrill for us was the privilege of seeing the Glen

Miller Orchestra, who played there several times while I was working with the CAVF. Never had I seen such a big band in my life or enjoyed music so much. On one occasion, I even played ping-pong with the red-headed trumpet player from the Glen Miller Orchestra and didn't even know who he was until he went up after our game and began playing in the band. Before going up on stage, he said, "Thanks for the good game," to which I responded, "Merci." Not only was he a good ping-pong player, but he was also a really good trumpet player.

On Sunday afternoons instead of going to the club, Solange, Raymonde, and I would go to the theater to see whatever production was available. On one particular Sunday, we got there early and chose some seats in the middle of the theater. Since I was on the outside with several empty seats beside me, I told Solange, who was sitting next to me, that I hoped no one came to sit beside us. The words had barely left my mouth when three young men wearing American uniforms decided to take the seats directly beside mine. Not thinking they would understand French, I told Solange in a rather rude tone of voice, "Why did these **Americans** have to pick **these** seats?" Much to my surprise and embarrassment, the American sitting beside me said in flawless, unaccented French (sounding like any Parisian I had ever met), "Miss, you really ought to be careful what you say. You never know who might understand." After my apologizing profusely, he introduced himself as Michel de Rothschild. He and his two buddies were interpreters for the American Army and spoke excellent French, although the other two did have a bit of an American accent. Before the show began, they introduced themselves to each of us, which was really nice because they could all speak with us in French.

When the show was over, they invited us to accompany them to the club for coffee and donuts. While there, we visited and really enjoyed the time we spent with these Americans who were able to talk to us. It turned out that Michel was so accomplished in French because he'd been born and raised in Paris and had only gone to America when the war started. The other two Americans, one from Chicago and the other from Boston, were very tall. While we visited, I learned that Michel's mother was English while his father was part of one of the wealthiest families in France. Unlike me, his childhood was filled with nannies and a great deal of formality. Even in speaking with his own parents, he was required to use the formal form of "you" rather than the familiar. Hearing stories of his childhood, I told him that I had grown up very poor, but that I thought my childhood had been far better than his and I wouldn't trade places with him for anything. Listening to him made me realize that money was not nearly as important as love.

They also were curious about our uniforms, so we explained that we each had served in the French Underground and were now working with this organization to help repatriate prisoners. Very interested in what we had to say, they listened as we described what each of our jobs entailed and what our responsibilities were. Every other Friday night at our hotel we were allowed to invite one guest, so we each asked one of these French-speaking Americans if they'd like to join us for dinner the following Friday. Although they were all very nice and very polite, Michel amazed me on that Friday when he showed up for dinner. It is a French custom to bring something when invited to dinner, and Michel's arrival proved to be no exception. After hearing how wealthy his family was, however, I was amazed when he pulled out a single Hershey bar and said it was for the three of us to share. Naturally, I thanked him for his gift and said nothing to show my surprise at his lack of generosity. The other two gentlemen offered us cigarettes, which we gladly accepted since we all smoked. On one other occasion, I went with Michel to the theater and was pleasantly surprised when he paid for both tickets. Shortly afterward, they left Paris, and Michel wrote to me several times. In one of his letters, he suggested that I come to visit his home in America. I laughingly told Solange and Raymonde that he probably wanted me to be a maid in his palace what with my poor background. At that point, I decided it might be best if I quit writing to him.

In the Hotel Lutecia, the lower level had been set aside to display photographs of people who had been taken prisoner during the war and had not yet returned. In this way, families could ask the whereabouts of their loved ones without having to stand in the lobby every day as the prisoners walked by. Since I had not heard from my missing family members, I attached their photographs as well in the hope that someone returning might be able to give me some news about them. Every day there were trainloads of prisoners coming in, which kept us extremely busy, but also gave me the hope that I would learn something soon.

The first news I had of anyone in my family came shortly after meeting Michel de Rothschild. I had just taken over a shift when a man came up to me and handed me a slip of paper with the name Hirsch on it. At my school every Friday Dr. Hirsch would come to check the children and give us any medicines deemed necessary to ensure our health. In addition this same Dr. Hirsch had served as the Boy Scout leader for my cousin Maurice, and his sisters had been the leader of the Girl Scout troop to which I belonged. Like many of the prisoners who returned, this man had no hair and really didn't look like the Dr. Hirsch I remembered from my childhood. Despite my fears that this man was a stranger, I asked him if he happened to be a doctor. To his affirmative response, I asked if he'd been a Scout leader called Gigot. Again he said that he had. To further verify, I asked if his sisters had been Scout leaders, too, and while nodding affirmatively, he asked who I was. I told him I was Cecile Widerman, who had lived on Rue des Deux Ponts. Showing that he remembered me, he asked about my cousin Maurice. At that time, Maurice was a prisoner of war, and we were expecting him to return soon. When he said that was good news, I gave him further good news. His two sisters had come through just the day before and had asked if I'd seen him. Until that time, he had no idea if they had survived or where they might be. Although he was thrilled with that news, he let me know that his wife and children had all died in a concentration camp. I took care of his papers and gave him a room to rest, showing him where the telephone was where he could call his sisters. Although I would have liked to spend more time with him and see him reunited with his sisters, there were many more prisoners who needed to be processed, so I had to leave him and go back to work.

Just a few days after seeing Dr. Hirsch, I worked the morning shift and was waiting for Solange to be replaced so we could go to visit with Marie France, a lady who had worked with the CAVF, but had quit because she adopted a baby and needed to be home with him. While waiting by the door, I heard an announcement on the loudspeaker requesting everyone to remain in the building because a big shipment of prisoners had just arrived and everyone would be needed to help with the processing of so many. Knowing Solange would not be coming and I would be needed, I waited for instructions as to what I should do. Several prisoners began passing by me, and as usual, I carefully searched every face to see if anyone from my family might be there. I could not believe my eyes when I saw what had to be my brother Robert passing along with a group and talking with several of the other prisoners. My voice caught in my throat, and I couldn't call to him. Since he did not see me, he kept on walking and visiting with his friends. Just as he was about to disappear into another room, I managed to scream out, "Robert!" All the Roberts in the entire group, and there were several, turned to see who had screamed.

Once he caught sight of me, my brother ran to my arms, and

we grabbed each other as we kissed and cried. We couldn't let go of each other. He kept touching my face and asking me if he were dreaming or if it was really me. I'll admit that I probably looked a lot different to him. Here I was in uniform, and I had dyed my hair an ash blonde, but he saw in my eyes that it was really me. After being on my own with no news of the family with whom I'd been so close for so long, I could hardly believe he was really there and could not let him go. Finally, he introduced me to his three friends. Henri was another young Jewish boy who had lost everyone in his family. Yves Darrier and Claude Francis Boeuf were two Frenchmen who had taken him under their care when he got to Buchenwald and helped to restore his health. He told me that if it hadn't been for these two, he would not have survived. Naturally, I was thrilled to meet them.

While we still held onto each other, I told Robert I had some good news for him. I told him that Jacques was still in Paris and had never been bothered. In addition, Fanny and her husband and two daughters were there. Henri, who had been in the French Underground, was back in Paris. Because he'd had two little girls, they let him return to his family instead of becoming a member of the military and going on toward Germany. Aimée was still there and was waiting for Gaston to return from prisoner-of-war camp. The best news of all was that Madeleine was safe and was now married to Jean Wegier. At this news, he told me that he'd been certain that everyone in the whole family was dead and he felt so thrilled to find that he wasn't the only one surviving.

Since they were all hungry, I took them to the dining room and told them I would begin processing their papers while they ate. Before doing any paperwork, I went straight to the telephone and called my brother Jacques. Since he didn't have a phone in his apartment, I called the café nearby and asked the proprietor to go get him for a very important phone call. Once he was on the phone, I asked him to guess who I had with me. He very angrily said that he couldn't guess and that I should just tell him. When I told him it was Robert, he replied that he didn't believe me and that it was too cruel a joke to be playing on him. I assured him it was no joke, but he insisted that I get Robert and put him on the phone, despite my telling him that he was eating and could call later. Jacques wouldn't hear of it, so I dragged Robert away from the food and his friends to come talk to Jacques. Before we got off the phone, I assured Jacques that I would bring Robert to his apartment as soon as I was finished with my job. Since Robert refused to leave Henri behind, I told Jacques that a friend would be coming with him. Jacques assured me that I could bring whoever as long as I was bringing Robert. Both Robert and Henri stayed with Jacques for about a month before managing to reestablish their lives.

That night both Claude and Francis stayed at the hotel and tried to contact their wives. The next day, the four of them met back at the hotel to have physicals and complete their paperwork. Needless to say, I did not go with Solange when my shift was over, but sent my apologies to Marie France instead. Naturally, she was thrilled that I had found my brother.

CHAPTER 15

The Magic of Music

Since Robert had always been the darling of our family, his return brought great joy to all of us who had managed to survive and return to Paris. When he'd first come back, his health was still a bit tenuous, but Jacques and Gaby soon had both Robert and his friend Henri feeling physically back to normal in no time. Robert had let us know that he and our brother-in-law Jacques had been separated from our parents, sister, and nephews who were sent to Auschwitz. He and Jacques, along with all the other men who were working age, were sent to a work camp where he had to put soles on boots. Because life there was so miserable, one day Jacques had asked Robert to sing, just to bring back some memories of when life was normal to help them cope with the life they were forced to endure at the work camp. He was overheard by the girl-friend of one of those in charge who liked his singing and brought him to the attention of her boyfriend. They both enjoyed his singing so much that every time there was a roll call to single out those to be shipped elsewhere, Robert and Jacques, too, would be set aside so they wouldn't be chosen. As a result, he was certain that it was entertaining that had helped him survive. Singing and dancing was all he wanted to do now that he was home, and he asked us not to ask him any more questions—he just wanted to forget the past and move on to the future. It didn't take him long to find employment in the entertainment industry. The one thing I was able to do that really upset him was go to the clubs and see the American bands without having to pay anything. He was especially jealous when I told him I was going to see Glen Miller's band and made the point of letting him know I'd seen them several times before. Although Glen Miller himself had been killed in 1944, his band still performed at the USO clubs that I was allowed to enter because of my uniform.

Our joy at having Robert back was tempered a bit after a few weeks. One afternoon I saw a girl from my school who told me she'd been in concentration camp during the war and was the only one in her family who had survived. Although that news brought me sadness, it was news of my sister Hélène that just about devastated me. Just as I'd done with everyone who had come back, I asked her if she'd seen Hélène or heard any news of her. Like everyone else I'd asked before, she said she had not seen Hélène, but she'd inadvertently heard news of her. One day while she was in camp, she heard a Polish girl singing a song that Robert had made up and taught to all of us. Knowing that only those of us from Rue des Deux Ponts would know that particular song, she asked the girl where she'd learned that song. Her response was that a French girl she'd met in another camp was always singing it, and it had stuck in her mind. My classmate then asked the girl to describe the French girl, and her description made it clear that the singer had to be Hélène.

Imagine my excitement at finally getting some news of Hélène. Of the hundreds I'd asked, no one knew anything until this one incident. Eagerly I asked if the girl had said anything else, if she knew where Hélène might be. Not only could I find it hard to believe what she had to say, but I also basically refused to believe her. According to the Polish girl, they had taken Hélène to the infirmary or clinics and she had never returned. Enough people had returned with horror stories to let me know that what she meant was that Hélène had been chosen for medical experimentation and had not survived the experience. My mind refused to accept that my beloved sister would never come back. There was no one in the family, no one that I ever knew, who was as strong and independent and full of life as Hélène. It just could not be possible that her life was over in such a way as this classmate described. I was certain that Hélène would have fought and brazened her way through anything. In my mind, my sister was a superhero, and superheroes just didn't die. Of all my family who had been taken, Hélène was the one I was certain would return. As it turned out, Robert, my small, young brother, was the only member of our family who returned from concentration camp. Despite my not wanting to believe what I had heard, I finally understood that nightmare of my father's telling me I could not come where they were. Of the thirteen members of my immediate family from France, Robert was the only one to return from the concentration camps. It wasn't until almost forty years after the war that I learned what had happened to my two sisters who had remained in Poland. On a visit back to Paris to see family, I met Shoshana and Sarah, the two granddaughters of my sister Sarah. According to them, their mother was the only one in her family to survive. She and her father and two of her siblings had left Poland and safely made it to Russia, but her father and her siblings went back to Poland to get her mother (my sister) and her little brother. Once they arrived in Warsaw, the ghetto was closed and they had all died there, along with my other sister Régine and her family. Sarah's daughter had immigrated to Israel after the war and lived there along with her two daughters, one son-in-law, and two grandsons.

Eventually, there were no more shipments of prisoners that

Claudine Lebouluec (*left*), Louisette Lebouluec (*to my left*), and their cousins.

needed to be processed, no more people to be reunited with family. Although our work was finished, the CAVF found jobs for many of us working with the Americans. I was assigned to an office that was in charge of looking up criminals of war. It was here that I met Claudine Lebouluec, a French girl from Orly. Her sister Louisette worked in a nearby office. By that time, my friends Solange and Raymonde had moved on to other jobs in other cities, so I would spend spare time with Claudine and Louisette, again going to the clubs and dancing to the great American music. Although the office work was interesting, it didn't last very long. The Americans decided to move this particular operation to Germany, so my job there was finished.

Needing a job and a place to stay, I went to visit Mariette, my nephew Jean's wife. Jean's parents had owned a bakery before the war, and Mariette was trying to run the bakery by herself while Jean was away in the army. She gladly let me move in with her and help out in the bakery. Although I worked in the bakery, I still maintained my friendship with Claudine and Louisette, who would come into Paris from Orly during their spare time to visit and go to the clubs. Not long after this, Madeleine and Robert managed to get my parents' apartment back, and I moved in with them. Although it was good to be home, it was very different living there with Madeleine, her husband, Jean, and my brother Robert. No longer were my father's machines by the window busily earning a living for the family. No longer was my mother in the kitchen cooking those wonderful meals that we had all taken for granted. Perhaps the biggest gap was the absence of Hélène, with whom I'd shared a bed in that apartment for as long as I could remember.

Just about the only thing that took my mind off what I had been through and what I had lost was to go dancing. Even though the war was over, there were still many soldiers from America, Canada, England, and a few other places stationed either in Paris or at Orly Field outside Paris. Nearly every day after work I would go with some friends to one of the clubs to dance. Some of the Americans were obnoxious and rude, only learning the most crude French expressions and acting as if all French women had no moral character. I usually didn't have any problems with these disrespectful men because I would almost immediately let them know I did not speak English and was only interested in dancing. Once I said that, they would focus on dancing and not try to talk to me at all. Although I may have been short and not exactly slender, I was a good dancer. As a result, I rarely danced an entire dance with the same partner. When the young men would see how well I danced, they would practically line up to tap on the shoulder of my partner in order to get to dance with me. To me, it didn't matter who my partner was, just as long as I got to dance.

Not only were there clubs where I could go to dance, but the synagogues also sponsored dances. One Sunday night before Mother's Day, I went to the dance at a synagogue with a friend, Marcelle. Although many of the soldiers were Americans, they were also Jewish and spoke Yiddish, so I was able to communicate with them. After we'd been there dancing for a while, they announced a dance contest. The prize for the soldier would be a telephone call home to his mother on Mother's Day. The girl who was his partner would receive five hundred francs. Although I'd danced with several young men before the announcement, one very good dancer asked me if I would be his partner for the contest. Since I loved to dance, I would have accepted any offer, but it was nice to be able to compete with a partner who could dance well. We had to dance several songs together while the judges dismissed the couples one by one, trying to select the best. When we won the contest, he thanked me over and over for helping him win the phone call to his mother. That was great for him, but five hundred francs was nothing to sneeze at, and I was just as happy for myself at winning such a large amount of money.

So far there had been several days in my life that I considered life altering—most of them for the worst. May 18, 1946, was another life-altering day for me, even though it dawned like many others and seemed to hold nothing of great importance. Since it was a Sunday, Claudine had invited me to come to Orly to visit with her family. Arriving early in the afternoon, I visited with Claudine and Louisette, along with their parents and other siblings. Shortly after my arrival, they suggested I stay for dinner and then accompany them to the American army base afterward to attend a dance that was to be held there. Since I had no other plans and I loved to dance, I accepted their offer, expecting this to be like the many other dances I had attended throughout the liberation and American occupation.

As usual, the music was great and there were many available partners who loved to jitterbug as much as I did. Shortly after our arrival at the dance, a very nice-looking American soldier came up to Claudine and asked her to dance. Already romantically involved with an American named Bill, Claudine turned him down, telling him she was waiting for her date to arrive. Still determined to dance, the young man turned to me and asked if I would like to dance. Dancing was the one great enjoyment of my life, and I cannot remember ever turning down an offer, regardless of what kind of music was being played. Not only was this young man very handsome, but he was also a good dancer. As we moved graciously around the room to "Laughing on the Outside, Crying on the Inside," something happened that made this one dance different from the hundreds of others I'd danced over the years. Much of the time, I had numerous partners during one song because the guys would see that I was a good dancer and would cut in. This time, as the guys moved toward us to cut in, I would shake my head negatively, and we would dance away from any guy who tried to cut in. Dancing with this young man was very nice, and I really didn't want to dance with anyone else.

When the music stopped, instead of taking me back to the table, he held my hand waiting for the next song to start. For that entire evening, I only danced with this one American. Never before had I gone to a dance and had only one partner. In fact, I could not remember ever dancing an entire song with just one partner except for the guy with whom I'd won the dance contest. Fortunately, Claudine and Louisette could speak English, and during breaks between songs would serve as our translators. I learned that my partner was a Texan named Bruce Holland, not an easy name for me to pronounce since the French have a unique way of saying "r" and never pronounce the "h" at the beginning of a word. Try as hard as I might, I could not pronounce Bruce, a name I'd never heard before. Finally, I learned his middle name was Edward, so I called him Eddie instead. Although not tall by most standards, at five feet, eight inches he was much taller than I, who didn't even manage to reach five feet unless I wore big platform shoes. His dark wavy hair helped to make his hazel eyes sparkle. Not only was he nice to look at, but he was also very polite and seemed a bit shy or quiet—not a bossy, boisterous, obnoxious American. Many of us French girls had encountered that type of American who had only bothered to learn the French words to ask someone to go to bed with them. Because of this, I had always enjoyed the fact that my partners were so numerous. I could just enjoy dancing without having to fend off unwanted advances.

Perhaps that is why I amazed myself at enjoying dancing with just this one man. I could have let him know I wanted to dance with others, but on that night, with that man, I had no thoughts of dancing with anyone else. In fact, we danced for so long that the train to Paris had quit running for the night. Since it was after midnight, my only means of returning to Paris was a bus, provided by the Americans, but in order to ride it, passengers either had to be American or be accompanied by an American. Fortunately for me, Louisette asked my special partner if he would accompany me on the bus back to Paris since the trains had stopped service and I had no other way to get home. Although he didn't speak French and I didn't speak English, somehow we managed to communicate at least to a small degree.

When the bus stopped near my home, he got off with me and walked me all the way to the door of the apartment building. Although I had never kissed anyone on a first date, there was something very different about this man. He'd been so nice to take me all the way home and see that I was safe that I took his hand and led him inside to a secluded area under the stairwell. It just seemed right to thank him by giving him a goodnight kiss.

Little did I realize that this kiss would change my life forever in just as drastic a way as the other major events of my life had done, only this time instead of sorrow and loss, this change would bring the love of a lifetime. Before he left, we somehow managed to make plans to see each other the following day (or perhaps I should say later the same day since it was after midnight). Fortunately, he was scheduled to be off and would meet me at the bus stop where we had gotten off earlier to walk me home. I watched him walk away, still amazed by all the events of the evening and greatly looking forward to the next evening when I would see him again. As I walked up the stairs to my apartment, I realized that I'd already made plans to meet Claudine to go to a movie the next afternoon. Before I went to sleep, I decided that somehow I'd just have to make both dates.

CHAPTER 16

With Love from Texas

On Monday afternoon, I made my way to the bus stop at Place Vendome where I had agreed to meet "Eddie," hoping I could get him to understand that I was supposed to meet Claudine to go to a movie and that he would agree to go along with the two of us. Apparently, he had just decided I would not show up because he had begun to walk away when I called out to him. The smile he greeted me with let me know that he was just as glad to see me again as I was to see him. Somehow, I managed to get him to follow me to the movie where Claudine was waiting for me. I was really glad that her mother, an English teacher, had taught both her daughters to speak fluently since she could explain to him about the movie and his going with us both. With one of us on each of his arms, he walked us over to the American cinema where we watched a movie that they both understood while I read the subtitles.

After the movie, we accompanied Claudine back to the train station where she caught the train for Orly. Before she left, Eddie told her to tell me that instead of taking the bus to come see me, he had hitched a ride with a friend who was coming to Paris. He'd been so eager to see me again that he didn't want to wait for the bus. As a result, he'd gotten there early and had paced back and forth, half afraid that I wouldn't show up. When she translated all this to me, I was very pleased to learn that he really wanted to see me again. Once Claudine left on the train, we walked hand in hand to one of the clubs that provided coffee, donuts, and music and sat there trying to talk to each other while we enjoyed our coffee and donuts. Before he left me at my apartment building that night, I understood that he planned to come back to my apartment to visit the next time he had a day off. Once again before he left, we went under the stairwell for a goodnight kiss that felt just as special as that first one.

After that, every time Eddie had a day off, we would meet. Sometimes I would go to Orly to meet him there, but often he would come to Paris. I got a French/English dictionary, and by looking up a word here and a word there, we managed to talk to each other. Quite frequently we would be with Claudine and/or Louisette, who could translate for us. By this time Louisette was very seriously involved with an American named Bill Kluge from Racine, Wisconsin, so we didn't see her as often. Whether we were in Orly or Paris, we would go to the club and dance or go to a movie or sometimes just walk hand in hand through the streets of Paris.

Before I started seeing Eddie regularly, I would go visit with my older sister Aimée, often having dinner with her at least once a week. After Eddie and I started dating continuously, I quit going to Aimée's for dinner, going out with him instead. Finally, after about a month of my not coming to dinner, I saw Aimée for the first time. She wanted to know what she had done to make me quit coming to visit. When I explained that she'd done nothing, but that I'd been dating an American, she insisted that I bring him over to dinner so she could meet him. It was not a custom for us to bring a date home to meet the family unless things were

BRENDA HANCOCK

very serious, but Aimée insisted on meeting this man who had taken me away from our visits. Fortunately, Aimée could speak English, too, so when I brought Eddie to her apartment for dinner, she was able to talk with him. Her husband, Gaston, and their daughter Sylviane and I all sat around not understanding while they talked, but then he didn't understand when the rest of us talked either. Despite the difficulties of the language barrier, that first dinner with someone from my family went very well. My sister Aimée was such a sweetheart and so was Eddie, so I knew all would be well. She let me know before we left that she really liked this young man and approved of my seeing him.

On one occasion when we were waiting in line to go into the Olympia, Eddie saw one of his best buddies also waiting in line. Dave Alton from Ohio was the first of Eddie's many friends for me to meet. Since he was Eddie's best friend, we made arrangements for him to meet my friend Marcelle, and after that, we would often go as a foursome to the clubs or movies. Even though Dave and Marcelle were just friends and never felt any romantic attraction, the four of us enjoyed going out together.

Eddie (Bruce Holland) and me, September 1946.

The first indication I had that things were getting serious between us, other than the way I felt about this quiet, polite, nice, handsome young American, happened one day when we were with Louisette. He told her to tell me that he wanted to meet my older brother Jacques. Before translating, she explained to him that in France, a young man didn't go visit with a family unless he was serious about the young lady in question. Despite what she said, he insisted that she ask me to set up a time for him to meet my brother. At about this same time, I began to worry about the day he would leave to go back to America. I knew a great emptiness would descend upon me once he was no longer there to walk along the streets holding my hand or dance with me or kiss me.

By the time July was nearing its end, I had decided that I needed to quit seeing him. I knew it would be hard enough to say goodbye at this point. If I continued to date him, I was sure that my feelings would only grow, and losing him would be just as difficult as losing all those members of my family that I had loved and lost. That evening after I'd made my decision, I told him we needed to quit seeing each other. In response he said that he insisted he see my older brother. Since I understood this to mean he wanted to marry me, I told him that I couldn't marry him for two reasons. The first reason was that I was older than he was, and the second was that I was a Jew and he was not. His response truly surprised me. He said, "Who cares?" Although he didn't actually say, "Will you marry me," it became clear to me that he was asking me to marry him and go back with him to America. Although I'd told him I was a Jew, from the time I'd left Paris in 1942, I had no longer considered myself a Jew. Like many my age who had lost so much, I questioned the existence of God. How could God let my wonderful mother, my adorable nephews, my beloved sisters, and even my stern father suffer so? My family might be Jewish and I wanted Eddie to know that, but I no longer felt Jewish, no longer believed in the God of my youth. On August 4, 1946, he surprised me by giving me an engagement ring. Only later did I realize the significance of the date. The last time I saw my parents had been on August 4 just four years earlier.

Finally, the day came for Eddie to visit with my brother Jacques. When we walked in, my brother's first response was to ask, "What are you bringing an American to me for?" I replied that I thought he wanted to marry me and was there to ask Jacques for permission. He surprised me when he answered, "You're old enough to marry. You don't have to ask me." Then, in order to accept him into the family, Jacques offered him a drink and managed to ask him what he wanted. When Eddie said that water would be fine, my brother exclaimed, "Water? Water is to wash the feet!"

About that same time, Eddie had written home to his parents for permission to marry me. Since he was only nineteen years old, he was not old enough to marry without written consent of his parents. His mother's first response was to remind him that the last thing she had said to him before he left for France was, "Son, whatever you do, don't bring home one of those French girls!" to which he had replied, "Aw, Mom, don't worry. I won't." Despite his earlier promises, he was so insistent that he told his parents if they refused to sign the permission forms, he would reenlist and stay in France until he was twenty-one and old enough to marry without their permission. Still, they were a bit skeptical. It was only after they'd gotten a report from Eddie's commanding officer and the chaplain, both of whom interviewed me before giving their consent, that they agreed to sign the papers. Apparently, they realized that I was not a gold-digger bent on marrying any American just so I could get a free ride to the United States, and they also knew how much Eddie loved me. The one thing they were not sure of at the time was that my love for him was just as great.

During my interview with the commanding officer and the chaplain, I learned that there were many French girls wanting to marry American soldiers. When the commanding officer had closed the door to begin the interview with me in the room alone, I did not expect him to try to seduce me. Although I didn't slap him as I wanted to, I let him know right away that I didn't want anything to do with him. Only after I had passed the "test" did he let me know that there were some girls he interviewed who took him up on his offer, thinking to get someone of higher rank and greater wealth. Not only during the interview, but also when he saw us together, he could tell that our feelings for each other were the real thing. Both he and the chaplain wrote in their letters that I was a fine young woman who truly cared about their son.

By the time Eddie and I were engaged, my sisters Aimée and Madeleine and my niece Mariette were all pregnant. Their husbands had returned from the war, and their reunions had all been quite productive. In late August I was called to the hospital where Aimée was about to deliver her baby. Because I was still wearing my CAVF uniform, they let me in to see her. Before I got to her room, I could hear her screaming. Apparently, the baby had died at four in the afternoon, but Aimée suffered through labor until the next morning before the baby was actually delivered stillborn. I was horrified at her suffering as well as at her loss. By the time I met with Eddie later that day, I took his ring off my finger and thrust it at him, saying that I did not want to marry him any more and that I never wanted to have any babies. Somehow, I managed to let him know of all the suffering I had just witnessed and how horrible it had been for my sister to lose her baby. As he kissed away my tears, he assured me that it was different in America. I don't know how he knew, but he told me that in America they put you to sleep and you wake up with a baby. I loved him so much and trusted him so much that I took the ring back.

BRENDA HANCOCK

Eddie, or Bruce as I began trying to call him since all of his friends called him that, got his first taste of a French wedding when he accompanied me to the wedding of Louisette and Bill. In France, two weddings must take place before the marriage is considered legal—a civil ceremony as well as a religious one—and Bruce and I attended both. After the ceremonies, her family gave her a big party to celebrate. The oldest of seven children, Louisette had two younger brothers, ten-year-old Milo and eight-year-old Michel, who both got drunk as a skunk at the party. Michel kept coming up to Bruce and me and telling me not to marry Bruce because he wanted me to marry him. We all laughed, and years later when I saw Michel as a young man, I teased him and asked if he still wanted to marry me.

Several things went into the preparations for our wedding. First, we had a small engagement party with Bill and Louisette and Claudine and her boyfriend, Bill Tuttle, and Bruce's best friend Dave. It was a very happy occasion with the wine flowing and everyone celebrating. Since most Frenchmen take August off for vacation, none of my family was in town to join the party. Shortly after that, he moved into the apartment with us, sleeping in the room with my little brother. One morning my brother walked into the kitchen carrying one of Bruce's socks. Showing me a hole in it, he said, "Look at what your fiancé is wearing! You need to mend his sock!" So, I did as my mother had taught me and darned the sock perfectly. When I handed it to him later, he asked me why on earth I had done that since he'd planned to throw it away. He was so impressed with my stitching that he said he was going to keep it to show to his mother.

Since Henriette's father was a tailor, he offered to make my wedding suit for the civil ceremony as my wedding gift from them. Even though I'd seen Willie again in Paris after I'd returned and before I'd met Bruce, I knew there was nothing really serious between us, despite Henriette's always insisting we were engaged.

Wedding photo—October 5, 1946. *From left:* maid of honor Marcelle, Bruce, me, best man Dave Alton.

The crazy thing was that Henriette's mother had not really approved of me as Willie's fiancée until Willie became interested in a Catholic girl. I supposed she decided I was much preferable to any Catholic girl because while Bruce and I had gone for a fitting, she came into the room and asked her young son, who was about eight years old, "Who is Nick going to marry?" She had obviously been prompting him earlier because he replied, "Willie!" Very quickly, I told him that this young man with me was the man I was marrying, not Willie. No matter how much I might have cared about Willie at one time, I was certainly glad I would not have his mother as my mother-in-law after that little experience.

Just like Louisette, I had two marriage ceremonies as well,

BRENDA HANCOCK

both taking place on October 5, 1946, just five days before Bruce's twentieth birthday and a little over a month before my twenty-fourth birthday. The civil ceremony took place at 11:00 in the morning at the mairie or courthouse near where I lived, with members of my family in attendance. The second ceremony was at 2:00 in the afternoon on base in the chapel with a Baptist minister officiating. The chaplain we had met and interviewed with earlier had been a Methodist minister who was very kind and helpful, and I hoped he would be the one performing the wedding. I wasn't really prepared for this minister, and I don't think he was quite prepared for me. Not only did my family attend, but Dave was there as Bruce's best man, and Marcelle stood up for me as my maid of honor since Suzanne could not come up from Montauban. Six more of Bruce's buddies were there as well, and I later learned that all six of them, as well as Dave, had tried to convince Bruce that he should not marry me, that he'd be better off finding an American girl when he got back home. Since nothing they said convinced him to change his mind, they all decided to show their support for him by coming to the wedding.

In most instances a wedding is supposed to be a serious affair, but mine was interrupted by peals of laughter. This minister, whom I was not expecting and apparently who didn't know that I didn't speak much English, turned to me during the ceremony and said a long, involved sentence that didn't make any sense at all. I later found out this was when he was asking me if I pledged to love, honor, and obey Bruce until death parted us. Instead of saying, "I do," my response was, "What you say?" The six guys burst into laughter at this, making our wedding quite different from most others. Apparently, at some point I managed to say the things I was supposed to say to make our marriage official because before long we were all ushered outside the chapel for a family photo.

Back in Paris my two aunts had spent days preparing a feast

November 1946—Newlyweds Bruce (Eddie) and Nicole Holland.

to celebrate the wedding. When we got back to our apartment, we found flowers everywhere and enough food for us to eat for two days. My whole family had chipped in to pay for the wedding, and they all gave us money as wedding gifts as well, knowing that we could not take actual presents back with us to Texas. Because he was so happy at our finally being married, Bruce would kiss me just about every other minute or so. My nephew Jean and his wife, Mariette, teased us about this and began counting between the kisses and saying things like, "Here comes another one!" My brother-in-law Jean was sitting near Mr. Lebouluec and kept filling his glass with wine before it could ever get empty. I know that I was beaming because many of the women there kept talking about how handsome my new husband was and how lucky I was to catch such a good-looking man. My smiles were because I knew that his heart was just as beautiful as his face was. After several hours of celebration, Bruce asked me if we couldn't go for a walk so we could be alone. Walking hand in hand down the Seine River around Notre Dame in the evening, I was filled with joy at being Mrs. Bruce Holland. When we got back to the apartment, everyone had gone except for Aimée and Gaston. Aimée was upset with me for our having left because everyone had wanted to say good-bye and we were gone without a word. I knew the family would all be back the next day to help eat up all the food and celebrate more, so I didn't see what difference it had made whether we were there or not.

CHAPTER 17

A New Home

From October through November of 1946 Bruce and I shared the apartment I had grown up in with Madeleine, Jean, their daughter Christiane, who was born October 30, and Robert. Bruce and I had the bedroom I had shared with my sisters when I was younger. Madeleine, Jean, and Christiane had my parents' bedroom, while Robert's bed was in what used to be our dining room. Since I was married to an American, I could buy groceries at the commissary on base where things weren't quite as expensive. Another benefit was that the commissary seemed to have everything; whereas, we'd been used to living with shortages for years. Even having to share with so many others, we were very happy just being able to be together all the time, except for when Bruce had to go to Orly to work.

By the beginning of November Bruce was told that he would be sent back to the United States very soon. Bill Kluge was also given orders to return, along with the guys who had been Bruce's buddies. The worst news I received was that he would be sent to Germany before being shipped back to the States and that I could not go with him when he left. I took him to the train station in

Paris where he met with Dave and the rest of the guys in his company. While waiting for the train, we would walk back and forth along the platform with me crying the whole time. Bruce's buddies all tried to cheer me up, telling me not to cry because we would be together again soon. One of his friends, Vis, even took out his false teeth to make me laugh instead of cry. It was amazing to see such a young man with false teeth, but I still managed to cry and laugh at the same time. When the train left, I went to my brother Jacques' apartment for a little bit in hopes that I could get some comfort there. I felt really sick, and my throat hurt almost as much as my heart did from being so quickly separated from my new husband.

Within a few days of Bruce's departure I received news that I was to depart for Germany on December 3. Fortunately, Louisette had been given the same news, so I knew we would be traveling together. The day of our departure, she came to our apartment where my family had gathered to say good-bye. We couldn't linger because we had specific instructions to be at the Gare de l'Est, the train station from which trains went to the east. Although I had traveled throughout France by myself during the war, I was glad to have her company on this leg of our journey to America. Bruce and I had sent a box to his home that contained my parents' silverware that Jacques had managed to save from our apartment. Although originally there had been a service for twelve, Madeleine and I each took half, and these were what Bruce and I used. In addition to the silverware, the day after my parents were taken Jacques had managed to get a tablecloth my sister Sarah had made, along with a few other items of ours as well as some of Ida's things she had brought to my parents' apartment. He took all he could carry, but when he came back to get more, the concierge refused to let him back into the apartment. Because I'd been told there was a limit to what I could bring, I had to refuse a few of the other things of my parents that he tried to give me. That tablecloth and my clothes were all I managed to get into my suitcase.

At the station, we were met by the Red Cross, who accompanied the two of us and many other war brides who were also traveling to Germany to take the boat to America. By nightfall, the train had reached Frankfurt where we spent the night in the only hotel still standing. Louisette and I shared a small room and again were glad we had each other instead of having to share with strangers. The rest of the city had been devastated and not much progress had been made in rebuilding. Early morning brought the final leg of our trip with a walk past the rubble to the train station where we boarded another train, which took us to Bremerhaven where we were supposed to wait to be placed on ships. Louisette and I were thrilled to see Bill and Bruce waiting for us at the train station. Instead of being herded along with the other war brides, we left with our husbands and walked down the street arm in arm.

We hadn't walked far before we were stopped by MPs. It seems they thought we were German women trying to pick up GIs! Bill and Bruce quickly explained that we were their wives and had just arrived in town on our way to America. By the time I had arrived in Bremerhaven, all of Bruce's buddies had already shipped out for home, but he'd gone to everyone he could find to try to make arrangements to travel with me on the ship. By that time Louisette was pregnant and really wanted Bill to go with her, too. We waited anxiously to learn of our travel plans. Just one day before I was scheduled to leave, Bruce came in smiling and telling me that he'd finally done it—he would be traveling with me. Louisette wasn't so lucky. She had to wait for another boat, and Bill did not manage to go with her. Once again I realized how very lucky I was as I looked around me on the *Gorham,* the ship carrying me to America. The ship, full of war brides from all over Europe, with very few GIs aboard, left on December 11, 1946. Although we were on the same ship, Bruce and I did not share a room. Instead, there were big rooms with lots of bunk beds stacked on each other like a dormitory. In the bunk next to me was a woman from Switzerland who was very sweet, but it would have been nice to have Louisette there as well. Mainly, I was really glad Bruce was there with me.

Each morning Bruce would come to the door of my room to pick me up and take me to the deck where I would sit covered up on a chair. Since it was December, the weather was very rough, causing the ship to lurch up and down. I was so sick for the entire trip that I only managed to eat two meals during the week we were on board—the first meal before the ship left the dock and the last one served after it docked in New York. Perhaps I wouldn't have been quite so sick if I hadn't discovered that I was pregnant, too.

Because Bruce had shown no interest in Christiane when Madeleine brought her home from the hospital, I thought he was not interested in having children and was very worried at how he would react to the news that I was most likely pregnant. When I finally told him my suspicions, he was very happy and excited at the prospect of becoming a father. Surprised at his reaction, I told him that I'd been afraid to tell him, afraid that he wouldn't want a baby. He asked me what had made me think that, so I explained that he'd never even wanted to hold Christiane. Laughing, he said, "She was just a baby. This will be OUR baby. That's different."

By the time the boat docked in New York harbor, I honestly had thought I wouldn't make it. Never have I been so sick in my life as I was during that week crossing the ocean. If Bruce had not been with me to encourage me to go up on deck each day, I think I would have just stayed in my bed and died right there on the boat.

The morning we docked in the harbor, I was finally able to eat something without the fear of losing it. Even before breakfast, I felt so much better that I cleaned myself up. When Bruce came to the room to get me, he was really happy to see how much better I looked. After breakfast, we took a stroll on the deck of the ship. As we walked, we encountered a colonel whom I had seen each day while Bruce was away eating breakfast. He always said, "Good morning," to me as he walked by the chair where Bruce had left me. This morning when he met us, he said, "Well, I see you aren't feeling sick today. I'm glad you're looking better." Bruce looked at me in wonder since he'd never seen the colonel before and I hadn't mentioned his daily passing. He said, "What's going on?" so I told him about seeing the colonel every morning while he was gone to breakfast.

Since we could not leave the ship until customs had come aboard and checked all the papers, it was late in the afternoon before we arrived at Fort Hamilton. There was another French girl named Andrée, who was accompanied by her husband, Jack. The two of us had to stay at Fort Hamilton in New York while our husbands went to Fort Dix in New Jersey to be processed and given their discharge papers. During the two days it took for our husbands to return, Andrée and I went out into the streets in New York to see what this new country was like. Since it was just days before Christmas, there was an abundance of everything—things we hadn't seen in years in France because of the war. I saw a display of fresh prunes and couldn't resist, while Andrée bought a can of sweetened condensed milk. Amazingly to me, she drank the whole thing at one time, while I savored my prunes and tried to make them last as long as possible.

While walking in the camp one day, Andrée and I were stopped by an American lady and her daughter who were waiting to join her husband in Italy. Since Andrée spoke some English, she was able to answer the questions the lady asked—where we were from and why we were there. That lady invited us to dinner, and since we were not expecting to hear from our husbands, we accepted. Unfortunately, while we were gone, our husbands came to visit us. We had not left word with anyone as to where we were going, which caused great problems. When we came back to camp, Bruce and Jack were about to leave to go back to Fort Dix and were almost beside themselves with worry as to what had happened to us. Bruce told me not to ever do that again, first because he had been extremely worried and second because he wasn't sure when we'd be leaving to go to Texas and he needed me to be ready to leave at a moment's notice.

As it turned out, he was right in telling me to stay in the camp where he could easily find me because we left for Texas the next day. I began to realize how very big America is when we had to ride on a train for two days just to get from New York to Texas. Fortunately, we had a sleeping berth on the train and were able to sleep comfortably, although very close together. At ten in the morning of December 23, 1946, we arrived in Greenville, Texas, where we got off the train and prepared to catch a bus to Alba, the small town where his family lived. Since the bus would not depart until five in the evening, Bruce decided we should go shop for civilian clothes for him, since he did not want to go home wearing his uniform. After buying pants, a shirt, and a jacket, we went to a hotel where we could clean up and rest before the trip home. While we walked through the streets of Greenville, all I saw were men wearing cowboy hats, boots, and shirts. I turned to Bruce and said, "I see the cowboys. Where are the Indians?" My knowledge of Texas was limited to the movies I had seen that only had cowboys and Indians. From the movies I had learned that New York was the big glamorous city, Chicago was full of gangsters, Hollywood had its stars, and Texas had cowboys and Indians. Nothing else in America was known to me, and I soon realized that the movies had given me a very biased, limited view of my new country.

Another big shock to me was the meal we had at the hotel in Greenville. When the waiter had asked me what I wanted, I replied that I'd like a steak and French fries. He asked if I wanted a little steak or a big steak. Thinking in terms of the servings I'd been used to in France, I asked for a little steak. When he brought out the plate, it wasn't a plate, but a platter and the big, thick steak seemed to practically cover the whole thing! I thought that was enough food to feed an entire family! I'd heard Texas was big, but had no idea exactly how big things were in Texas.

After resting a while, we went to the bus station to catch the bus for Alba, his home town. The bus stopped in every little town along the way with my thinking at each stop that we were finally there. As the bus pulled into the town just prior to Alba, Bruce said that he knew we'd be there soon, and his heart was beating really fast—that he was nervous. I told him that I was very nervous, too, and couldn't imagine what my reception would be like. When the bus finally stopped in Alba, darkness had fallen. Bruce got off the bus first and was greeted by his father, who said, "Children?" His dad had come every day for a week to the bus station to wait for me since he'd been told I would be coming in accompanied by a Red Cross worker. They didn't know that Bruce would be with me or the exact day I would be arriving. Bruce answered, "Yes, Dad," as he helped me off the bus. My father-in-law welcomed me with a kiss and a hug without any reservations and helped us get our bags in the car. Surprisingly to me, he seemed to be trying to kiss me on the lips. In France, everyone greets everyone else with kisses, but always on the cheeks. It seems he and his other daughter-in-law, Mozelle, were in the habit of kissing on the lips, but I immediately turned my cheek to him. Kisses on the lips were reserved for Bruce alone!

After a short drive, we were home, an old one-story house that was decorated for Christmas. Although the house seemed very dark to me, my mother-in-law welcomed me with a hug and reached over to kiss Bruce. Later he told me that was the second time in his life that he remembered his mother kissing him. The first time was when he'd left to go to France. Although he knew she loved him, she was a reserved, nondemonstrative woman whose display of affection was usually limited to a pat on the back. Although the house was a bit larger than the apartment in Paris, it wasn't large, and the main thing I remembered about it was that it was very dark. Shortly after greeting us, my mother-in-law showed us to the table where she had dinner waiting for us. While we ate, I realized what it must have been like for Bruce all those times he had to endure everyone speaking French and his not understanding much. It had been a while since they'd seen Bruce, and they seemed to have lots of questions to ask him, trying to catch up on lost time. Although the food was very different, I enjoyed the meal and tried not to feel so out of place.

The next day was Christmas Eve and all of Bruce's family that lived nearby came over to meet me. My mother-in-law spent all morning cooking a huge Christmas feast to serve her two sons and their wives, as well as her daughter and her new husband. Sitting at the table were Bruce's brother Herbert and his wife, Mozelle, and their daughters Eluria and Sarah Jo, his younger sister Geneva and her husband, Armand, who had married just two weeks before we had, with Bruce and I seated by his parents, Nathan and Gertrude. Never in my life had I seen so much food on one table. Much to my amazement, they piled their plates high with everything that was available. In France, I'd been used to having just one thing brought to the table at a time. I'm almost positive they kept asking Bruce what was wrong with my appetite and wondered at my picking at the food. The meal had not been over long when a constant stream of neighbors dropped by. Word had gotten around the community that Bruce had just come back from overseas with his new bride, and they were all curious as to what a foreigner might look like. I felt like some prize cow as the townsfolk passed by, looking me over and saying things that I did not understand. I'm guessing things went well because Bruce was smiling the entire afternoon, never venturing far from my side.

While everyone visited, I just sat and took everything in.

From left: Gertrude Holland, Bruce, Nathan Holland shortly after returning from France, 1947.

Bruce's parents didn't look a thing like mine. His mother, unlike mine, was slender with salt-and-pepper-colored hair and skin roughened by days of working out in the sun. My mother's skin had been white and as smooth as a baby's. His father had thick, wavy hair that was turning white and a big, friendly smile. Even when my family and I had seen pictures of him in France, we all thought that he very closely resembled Harry Truman. His brother, Herbert, was taller and thinner than Bruce and not nearly as handsome, and Herbert's wife, Mozelle, was just about as thin as anyone I'd ever met. Even though I didn't think either of them was very attractive, they were very nice to me, and their daughters, who were five and nearly three, were cute little girls. Geneva and Armand were both very nice-looking young people. Armand towered over Geneva, who was several inches taller than I. Her gentle features were enhanced by her dark, curly hair, which matched Armand's and made them an attractive couple. They seemed very happy with each other and very willing to accept me into the family.

Christmas Day brought another huge meal and even more new people for me to meet. Since Mozelle's family lived in the same town, she and Herbert planned to eat at his parents' for lunch and hers for dinner. In order to welcome Armand to the family as well,

BRENDA HANCOCK

my mother-in-law told Geneva to invite his family to the Christmas lunch, which added his parents and two sisters. My father-in-law had either won or bought a huge turkey that was large enough to have served the entire town as far as I could tell. Since Armand's family also brought along food, I was amazed at the overabundance. Again, everyone seemed to be piling everything on their plates at once and practically diving in. The final straw came when my father-in-law place the biggest turkey drumstick I'd ever seen on my plate. I'm not sure if it was left-over seasickness, morning sickness, or what, but the sight of that leg made me so sick I didn't think I could eat anything. Fortunately, Bruce came to my rescue and told his father I couldn't eat that much and not everything on my plate at the same time. As he explained how the French people eat things one at a time, my father-in-law removed that giant drumstick from my plate. Again there were many new flavors for me to try, but I just couldn't eat very much.

Bruce explained to me that he had two more sisters, Erbie and Dee, who didn't live close enough to come for Christmas. His oldest sister, Erbie, lived in California where her husband, Cliff Harvey, served in the navy, surviving the attack on Pearl Harbor on December 7, 1941, and serving in the Pacific theater of operations throughout the war. His next oldest sister, Dee, lived in Eastland, a town in west Texas, with her husband, Pete Tindall. Pete was more like what I had seen in the movies, wearing cowboy boots, cowboy hat, and a big belt buckle. Not only did he have land, cattle, and sheep, but he was also a member of the sheriff's posse and had saddles and horses to boot. Shortly after Christmas Bruce and I took a train to Eastland in order for me to meet Dee and Pete and Dee's son Dean and Pete's daughter, Dorothy Helen.

Although it had rarely snowed in Texas, shortly after our arrival in Eastland, they had one of the biggest snowstorms in recorded history. They all teased me, saying that I had brought

Bruce, me, and nephew Dean in Eastland, Texas, right after Christmas 1946.

the snow with me from France. Dorothy Helen loaned me her cowboy boots in order for us to go out into the snow to take pictures. Because of the snow, we ended up stranded at Dee and Pete's and stayed longer than we had originally intended. Once again, the entire family made me feel truly welcome, even though I still couldn't communicate with them very well.

Because I wouldn't eat, Dee was very concerned about my health. Bruce kept telling her that I'd been really sick on the trip coming over and that I still wasn't feeling well. She insisted I go see the doctor to make sure I was OK and set up an appointment for me. Before we even got back to her house, she had called the

BRENDA HANCOCK

doctor's office to see what was wrong. As a result, she was the first of Bruce's family to learn that we were expecting a baby. She was also the first and only one for a while to know that I was Jewish. As soon as he had told her my maiden name was Widerman, she said, "She's Jewish, isn't she?" When he told her that I was, she let him know right away that it didn't make any difference to her. Taller than her little sister Geneva, Dee was as beautiful a lady as Bruce was handsome. She, too, had dark, wavy hair, a smooth complexion, and beautiful eyes that showed the world the tender heart she had in common with her younger brother.

Dee's son, Dean, was ten years younger than Bruce and Dean thought of Bruce as a big brother more than an uncle. When he was young, his allergies caused him to need to live with Bruce and his family. At ten years old, he was a really cute little boy who was bashful, but who obviously worshiped his uncle Bruce. Dorothy Helen still lived with her father and was just about Bruce's age. Very friendly, she was an outgoing young lady who could find the humor in any situation. She was the one who had taught Bruce how to dance, and for that I was forever grateful. Thinking back on all of Bruce's family, I realized that once again I was a very lucky young woman. This family welcomed me from the very beginning and treated me as well if not better than my own family had done.

From left: Geneva, Dee, Bruce, Erbie, and Herbert—Bruce and his siblings shortly after return from France.

CHAPTER 18

And Then We Were Three

When the snow finally melted, we took the train back to Alba to pick up our things and begin our new life together. First on the agenda was to decide where we would live. It was fairly obvious that we couldn't stay in Alba as there were no industries, no work for a young man to support his family. Geneva and Armand had already moved to Dallas. Bruce asked me if I would prefer to move to Dallas or Houston. Since I had no knowledge of either city, I asked him where they were located. When he told me Dallas was eighty miles from Alba and Houston was over two hundred miles from Alba, I told him I thought Dallas made more sense. We gathered our few belongings and took the train back to Dallas.

For the first couple of days in Dallas, we stayed with Armand and Geneva in the small house they rented. Most important was for Bruce to find a job. Fortunately for us, he got the first job he applied for and began working right away at the Dallas Medical and Surgical Clinic in the billing department. Since he'd been a teletype operator in the military instead of the tail gunner he'd originally planned to be, he had learned how to type, a much more useful skill than operating a gun. One of the benefits of his working there was free medical care for me during my pregnancy.

Next on the agenda was to find a place of our own. Once again luck was with us. Apartments seemed to be scarce, but just about the time we were afraid we wouldn't find anything, Bruce talked to his uncle Cleve, his father's brother. Uncle Cleve had a house that he'd made into three apartments. One of the apartments was occupied by his brother, Odie, who had gone to Oklahoma to work and was rarely home. Since Odie was never there, Cleve decided to let us rent the apartment instead for twenty dollars a month. Our apartment had a kitchen and one other room with bathroom facilities that we had to share with the tenants of the neighboring apartment. Fortunately, the apartment was furnished, and my mother-in-law had given us a skillet, a few plates, and a pan, which we used with the silverware that had been my mother's. The first thing we had to buy was an iron and ironing board so that I could take care of Bruce's clothes, and the first piece of furniture we bought was a baby bed. Since there was a phone in the hallway, Bruce would call me two or three times during the day. He knew that I didn't know anyone and couldn't talk to them if I did, so he would call to make sure I was feeling OK. Each time he would say, "You've been crying again, haven't you?" Then he would try to cheer me up before having to leave to go back to work. Much later he told me that if I had not been pregnant, he would have sent me back home to keep me from being so miserable. It tore at his heart to leave me all alone each day and see me so lonesome.

The first weekend after we'd moved into our apartment, we went to look for a car so that Bruce could drive himself to work without having to worry about streetcar schedules. Although he never liked it much, the dark blue Plymouth we bought turned out to be reliable transportation which got him back and forth to work and enabled us to go to Alba to visit his parents at least once a month until the doctors told me I should not travel any more.

Even before we'd left France, Bruce had told me of a friend of his from Texas that he'd met while training in the army and learned that they shared the same birthday. He and Don Bolden, this buddy, had gone AWOL together once in order for Don to go visit his young bride. Bruce often said that after we settled in, he would try to look up Don and Jean so they could meet me. One day in early February while Bruce was taking a break at work to get a drink of water, Jean saw him and asked Don if that wasn't his friend from the army. They had come into the clinic because Jean was expecting their first child. Very glad to see them, Bruce told them that he was married now, too, and was also expecting a baby. Before they left, he made arrangements for them to come to the apartment and meet me.

On the day they were scheduled to come, once again I felt really sick and was terribly cold as well. I had put on one of my dresses, but had put my bathrobe on over it and was resting on the bed, hoping to warm up and feel better when Bruce welcomed them into our apartment. What a beautiful couple they made! Jean looked like a little doll to me, wearing a light gray suit, a red hat, and red shoes and carrying a red purse. Her hair was as black as coal, while his was blond. She was so stunning that I barely looked at Don and felt even worse at lying around with my robe on. Not only was she pretty and seemed to represent a typical American girl, but she was very sweet as well. She complimented me on my robe and how pretty it was. I sat there listening to the three of them, but understanding very little of what they said. Amazing as it may sound, I could understand most of what Bruce said and the things I didn't understand, he could explain, but when several began to talk, I got lost in all the words. They seemed to have a very good visit, and Jean invited us to dinner on the following Sunday.

Unlike us, Don and Jean lived in a duplex with her aunt and cousins living in the other side of the duplex. Their apartment consisted of a living room, a bedroom, and a kitchen with their own bathroom that they didn't have to share with anyone else. After looking around their apartment, I sat there bored to tears because I still could not follow a conversation with several people talking. My boredom was interrupted when Jean invited her aunt and cousins to come over to meet us. Again, these people seemed to be very nice, but it would have been so much nicer if I had been able to understand them. My understanding of Bruce's situation in France grew with each day I spent in Texas unable to carry on a conversation.

Determined to remedy the situation, I began studying the newspaper. Because I was pregnant and we didn't have an abundance of money, I couldn't take language lessons. Fortunately for me, the alphabet for English and French was the same, so I got my dictionary and the newspaper that we subscribed to and spent my time learning to read. When I had questions that the dictionary didn't answer, I would ask Bruce what on earth that sentence or that word meant. The one word that gave me the most trouble was "meanwhile." I would see it in the comics all the time, but couldn't figure out what it meant. Finally, I asked Bruce, who did an excellent job of explaining and solving the mystery. Jean also helped me learn English. After that first Sunday, Jean and I would visit at least once or twice a week. Bruce showed me how to take the streetcar to get to Jean's apartment, and I would take my dictionary with me, glad to have a diversion to the lonely hours waiting for Bruce to come home from work. Jean and I had a lot in common since we both were expecting our first baby and were going to the same obstetrician. Not only would I visit with Jean during the day, but Don and Jean and Bruce and I often visited at night as well, taking turns cooking dinner. Most of the time our meals consisted of mashed potatoes, peas, and corn, along with some kind of meat. When I'd married Bruce, I didn't know how to boil water because my mother had always done the cooking.

By May, Jean and I were both showing our pregnancies, and the Texas weather was beginning to take its toll on me. Never before had I experienced such heat. One Sunday the four of us had gone to White Rock Lake, and since it was so hot and our feet had swelled so, Jean and I took off our shoes. They took a picture of me barefoot, which I sent to my sister Madeleine. When she got that photo, she wrote me back immediately asking if she needed to send me money for shoes. She thought we couldn't afford any shoes and didn't understand how very hot it was.

On July 21, 1947, after a very difficult labor Jean gave birth to a baby boy they named Roy Duane. One day before my child was born, Don and Bruce and I had been left to take care of Duane by ourselves. My first experience at changing a diaper happened that day. With both men watching carefully, I was a nervous wreck, afraid I would accidentally stick the baby with the diaper pin or not put the diaper on properly. Exactly two weeks later our daughter, Barbara Elaine, was born. Dr. Bourland, my obstetrician, asked me after I woke up from the anesthetic, "What did Jean tell you?" It seems that the entire time while I was in labor, I kept saying, "Jean tell me that." She had explained all she'd been through, so even in my groggy state as what she'd said happened, all I could say was, "Jean tell me that." Thank goodness for Jean.

Before she'd been born, Bruce had told me I could pick the name of our child. A Jewish tradition is to honor someone in your family who has died by giving his or her name to your baby. I told him I wanted to name the baby after my mother and sister if it was a girl. He told me that folks in Texas would call the baby Berthee Heleen if I spelled it Berthe Helene as they'd been spelled in France. Not wanting to shackle my child with such a horrible name, but still wanting to honor my mother and sister, I chose Barbara Elaine, especially since I pronounced the second name exactly as I had pronounced my sister's name. Although she was the most beautiful baby in the world to me, my mother-in-law let me know right away that she looked like a drowned rat! Since I had such difficulty getting used to my new diet, Barbara only weighed five pounds, seven ounces and was very long and skinny.

I had gained only eighteen pounds during the entire pregnancy.

Unlike many French war brides I later met and visited with, I was blessed with my mother-in-law. When I came home from the hospital, she came to stay with me for twelve days and helped to teach me how to take care of my new baby exactly as I had seen my own mother do for her children. Before I left the hospital, my doctor had given instructions for me to stay in bed for twelve days, telling Bruce that I wasn't a horse or a cow and I needed to take care of myself. My mother-in-law cooked, did the laundry, and took care of both the baby and me.

Bruce and daughter Barbara in 1947.

Although I missed my mother and wished she were there to help me, I greatly appreciated this wonderful woman who treated me as well as she did her own children.

CHAPTER 19

Four and No More

Having Barbara was probably the best thing that could have happened to me. Instead of sitting around the two-room apartment by myself after I'd finished cleaning, wondering how to pass the time until Bruce got home, I now had plenty to fill the hours. Although she was very thin at the beginning of her life, it didn't take me long to fatten her up. The pediatrician, Dr. Luecky, was amazed at the beautiful little girl we brought back for her one-month check-up. The biggest problem, at least for Bruce, was that I would not let Barbara cry. Although I would put her down in bed from time to time so I could get things done around the house, I would not let her cry at all. The minute she started crying, I would pick her up. As a result, at night she would want to be held, too. From time to time, when I was just too tired to stay awake, Bruce would stay up with Barbara. Working all day and helping with Barbara at night began to take its toll, and soon Bruce was the one who was too thin.

Jean's aunt and cousins, who still lived next door, would come over to play with the babies. They were thrilled to have not one, but two babies to play with again. By that time, I was able to visit

From left: me, Bruce, Don, and Jean on the twenty-first birthday of Bruce and Don.

and carry on a conversation, even when there were several people all talking at once. When I dressed Barbara up in a little sweater, hat, and booties that I had knitted for her, they all told me she was the most beautiful little girl, and I just beamed with pride.

Barbara was only ten months old when I discovered I was pregnant again. As soon as I knew, I called Jean and said, "Guess what." The first words out of her mouth were, "Don't tell me. You're pregnant! Oh, you poor thing!" How she knew was a great surprise to me. She tried to comfort me and assured me that she'd help the best she could when the new baby came. It was only two weeks later that Jean called me and said, "Guess what." Right away I knew that she was pregnant, too. Barbara was exactly two weeks younger than Duane, and now I was expecting a baby two weeks before Jean was expecting her second.

By that time, my sister-in-law Erbie had come to live in Alba with her mother because her husband, Cliff, was sent away on his ship for a tour of duty. Erbie, like her sisters before her, welcomed

BRENDA HANCOCK

me into the family. I might have lost my parents and several of my sisters, but I found equally loving parents and sisters in my husband's family. Three weeks before I was due, Erbie came to pick up Barbara and take her back to Alba where she and my mother-in-law took care of her while I awaited the birth of our second baby.

Since my younger brother's birthday was March 1, I wanted this second baby to be born on his birthday. Dr. Bourland had told me that my baby would be here March 6, but on the morning of the first, I began having pains and Bruce took me to the doctor. After checking me, Dr. Bourland turned to Bruce and said, "She's not ready yet. Bring her back on the sixth." Not only was he right about the date, but he'd also said I would have another girl and that Bruce could name this one. Although he wanted Beverly Kay, I couldn't say Beverly, no matter how hard I tried. We agreed that I would need to be able to call my child by her name, so he asked me if I could say Brenda. I will admit that the way I said it wasn't quite like everyone else, but I was able to say something that sounded somewhat like Brenda Kay. Secretly, I had hoped that Allen Edward, the name we had chosen for a boy, would be what we used, but Dr. Bourland was right—Brenda Kay was born early in the morning of March 6.

Once again I went to sleep during the delivery and was awakened by Bruce who told me that we had a beautiful baby girl, even prettier than Barbara. In my mind I couldn't believe that any baby could be prettier than my little girl, not thinking of Barbara as she had looked when she was born, but of her now. At nineteen months old, she had brown hair and brown eyes and was the most beautiful little girl I had ever seen. I didn't remember the skinny drowned rat that Barbara had been at first.

I shared a room with a lady who had also had a baby girl. When Brenda was a day old, my roommate's husband came into our room and told his wife that they had a beautiful baby, but that the baby next to theirs was even more beautiful and that her last name was Holland. His wife told him that I was Mrs. Holland and it was my baby that he was talking about. So, he turned to me and told me that my daughter was very pretty. Once I saw Brenda, I noticed the differences between her and her sister right away. Not only was she healthier looking than Barbara had been at birth, but she was also fair. Barbara looked more like Bruce's family with a skin tone that showed their American Indian heritage. Brenda was more like my family with lighter skin and blue eyes. Somehow, it turned out that all the Holland granddaughters had the same coloring with the older one having dark hair and eyes and the younger one with light hair and eyes.

When it was time for me to go home, Erbie came with an ambulance to take me back to Alba. Bruce followed in our car so that he could go back to work the next day. She and my mother-in-law had made arrangements for me to travel the eighty miles in the most comfortable way possible. We'd only been at my mother-in-law's house for a day when both Erbie and my mother-in-law got sick. Although I wanted to get up and help to take care of them, they both insisted I stay in bed while they made a phone call to Dee to come take care of us all. As soon as she could get packed and drive there, Dee showed up and took over the care of me, Brenda, Erbie, and my mother-in-law as well as look after Barbara. This time I stayed in bed only nine days, but in the couple of days that Dee had a house full of sick folks, we nearly worked her into a sickness of her own caused by exhaustion. The very first night Dee was there, she put Brenda in the bed and turned out the light. Brenda started crying as soon as the light went off. Dee turned the light back on, and Brenda quit crying. I told Dee to give her to me, intending to do with this baby as I had with Barbara and not let her cry. After about three tries to make sure it was just turning off the light that was making her cry, Dee, who was exhausted, said, "You little devil, you can just cry!" It didn't take very long for Brenda to quit crying. Dee's persistence paid off. Unlike Barbara whom I'd never let cry, Brenda learned right away that it was OK not to be held all the time.

Not only was Barbara glad to see me, but she seemed very excited about her new baby sister and often said, "Baby. Baby." This joy with her baby sister lasted the whole time we were in Alba because she received lots of attention from her aunts and grandmother. Once we were home and she realized that a lot of my time would be taken caring for this new addition, a bit of jealousy began to develop. Fortunately, Dr. Leucky knew exactly what to do and let me know that the reason Barbara was taking all of Brenda's toys away from her was that she wanted my attention. With the doctor's good advice, the problem was soon remedied.

After two weeks in Alba, Bruce took the four of us home and I learned that exactly two weeks after Brenda had been born, Jean had given birth to a little girl they named Donna Jean. In such a short time, we'd gone from two young couples with no children to each having two children and our hands full. Because we both were so very busy, our visits during the week were limited, mostly just grabbing a few minutes on the phone every now and then. On the weekends when our husbands were there to help, we still tried to get together often.

We hadn't been back in our apartment long before it became clear that the apartment was far too small for the four of us. Bruce learned that a new housing addition was being developed outside Dallas called Pleasant Heights. He and Armand went to the contractor and bought houses next door to each other. The house was larger with a kitchen/living room combination and a bedroom; however, it was lacking in many ways. First of all, there were no cabinets or any other amenities in the kitchen that set it apart from the rest of the house. There were just walls and electricity. In addition, there was no bathroom and no running water. Very quickly Armand and Bruce built an outhouse, but they still had to go into town to haul water back. Since it was springtime and it rained often, the streets were nothing but black mud. Any car that tried to drive all the way to the house would get stuck, so Erbie even ruined a new pair of shoes trying to come to see us.

Not only was the house hard to get to, but other things about living there were difficult as well. I had to use the dishpan to bathe the children, and bathing for ourselves wasn't easy either. Even as poor as my family had been in France, I had never been subjected to living without running water and the ability to clean my house, my clothes, and myself. I was miserable, and the children were suffering, too. Never in my life had I ever used an outhouse or been forced to cart in water that I had to boil before being able to use it. Although I tried to adjust, I finally wrote to my brother Jacques and told him how miserable I was and that I wanted to come home. I knew it would take time for my letter to get there and a response to come back, but I waited anxiously each day for a sympathetic response. When his letter came back to me telling me that I should stay where I was unless my husband beat me, drank excessively, cheated on me, or was in some other way unbearable, I was even more miserable. For the longest time I did not write to my brother again and was angry that he didn't sympathize at all, saying instead that I'd made my choice and needed to live with it regardless.

Whoever chose Pleasant Heights as the name of the housing addition certainly had different ideas about what was pleasant than I did. The final straw came one day when I didn't have any water left to make formula for Brenda. On that day, Bruce and Armand went for water and were gone a very long time. Brenda was crying because she was hungry, but there was nothing I could do until they got back with water. The longer she cried, the madder I got. By the time he got home, I could take no more. I told him that if he didn't find me another place to live that had running water and a bathroom, I would leave him. I planned to go to Dallas, get a

BRENDA HANCOCK

job, and work until I could save enough money to take the girls and go back to Paris. Of course, he was worried about selling the house, but he knew that I was serious about leaving, so he did his best to find something else as quickly as possible.

Within two days, Bruce had made arrangements for us to move into an apartment complex called Texan Courts. Most of the people living there had been in the army and were returning from service overseas. Finally, I had running water, a bathroom with a shower, and two bedrooms, along with a living room and kitchen. The streets were paved, and I felt as if I'd gone to heaven. Not long after we'd moved he managed to sell the house, and even though we didn't make a profit, I was never so happy as I was when we were no longer tied to that horrible place.

From left: Barbara, me, and Brenda in 1949.

CHAPTER 20

Totally American

One of the nice things about living in Texan Courts, besides having running water again, was the friends I met there. Since we'd moved, we hadn't seen that much of Don and Jean. It was just too hard for Jean and me to visit during the week like we used to since we both had two children. First, I made friends with the couple who lived two doors down. Jo and T. V. Abbott had a daughter, Eska Jean, who was just younger than Barbara and older than Brenda. The three little girls would play together while Jo and I visited, and we both counted on each other to baby sit if the need came up.

By this time, I also met a few other French ladies who lived nearby. When I took the girls to Dr. Leucky for a check-up one day, the nurse told me there was another French lady who brought in her little boy and asked if she could give my telephone number to her. A week later, I received a phone call from Yvette, and after talking for a while, I invited her to come for a visit, explaining that I had two children and could not easily go visiting. She and her husband, Vernon, came for a visit that weekend, leaving their son at home with her parents, who lived with them. Both

Bruce and I enjoyed visiting with them, the men discussing their experiences during the war, while Yvette and I talked in French. Before they left, they invited us to come visit with them and meet her parents. When we arrived at their house, not only were her parents there, but she had met another French lady from Paris whom she'd invited as well. We'd just met Yvette's parents when Hélène and Roy Britton came in and introductions continued. Naturally, French was flying around the house, and it felt so good to be able to speak French again. Fortunately for Bruce, Vernon and Roy were there to visit in English, and they seemed to be enjoying the visit as much as I was.

The most unfortunate thing about that visit and the two other visits we made to see Yvette and Vernon was the way her parents treated Vernon. Bruce understood enough French to know that they were constantly degrading him, calling him a pig, and telling their daughter how little they thought of him and how miserable they were to be away from France. It got so bad that I could not hold my tongue and told them that if I were as miserable as they, I'd go back to France. They had an answer for that, too. They'd sold everything to come join their only daughter and could not go back and start over again. Instead, they decided to be miserable and to let everyone know how much they despised America and their American son-in-law. After two more visits, Bruce said that we should never go back, and I agreed with him.

Although I really liked Yvette and Bruce liked Vernon, her parents caused us to see very little of them. After that first meeting of Roy and Hélène, Bruce and I both spent time with them. The best thing about my friendship with Hélène was that she had a car and could drive. Even though she had a son Philippe, who was also born between Barbara and Brenda, she could put him in the car and drive over to visit with me. When we first met, one of her aunts had come for a visit, so she and her aunt and Philippe came. It was almost like being back in France being around people who could talk with me in French. Hélène and I even discovered that we had gone ice skating at the same place on the same days in Paris as teenagers and thought it was amazing that we had to come all the way to Texas to meet.

One day when the milkman was delivering my milk, he told me that the lady who lived in the next complex over was from Belgium. Because I was so occupied with the girls, I did not go over to meet her, but one Saturday morning she came to visit me. It seems the milkman had told her that I was Mrs. France from Holland. Because she lived in Belgium, she knew both French and Dutch and was excited to know that even though the milkman had gotten it backward, she would still be able to talk with me. Yvonne Brandon was a very tall lady with a wonderfully sweet personality who lavished my girls with presents all the time. She worked at a major department store in Dallas and would constantly buy dresses and shoes and things she thought would look cute on Barbara and Brenda. After I introduced Yvonne to Hélène, the three of us became great friends.

Shortly after we moved to Texan Courts, Bruce got a job with Standard Brands delivering food products. The hours were about the same as his job with the Medical and Surgical Clinic, but the pay was considerably more. He still had weekends off and was home early every evening, which gave him time to play with the girls before they had to go to bed. Things were really looking up, and I shouldn't have had any problems at all. Unfortunately, no matter how happy Bruce and the girls made me or how much I enjoyed visiting with my French friends, the losses that I suffered during the war must have constantly been eating away at me. Maybe it was reminiscing with Hélène about our youth in Paris or just speaking French again that brought the inner turmoil to a head. I began to think I was going crazy. Every time I would look in a magazine or at a group photo in the paper, I was sure that I was seeing my sister Hélène in the crowd, that she had amnesia and didn't remember any of us. I couldn't accept that she was gone forever.

It got to the point that I would have spells where I couldn't talk and I would run out of the house in fear. Barbara would run after me calling, "Mamma! Mamma!" The only words I could get out of my mouth were, "Go home!" I felt I was going insane. Bruce was equally scared and did everything he could to baby me and make me feel safe. Several times he would take me to my doctor to see if something could be done, but the doctor couldn't find anything wrong. Days would go by with nothing feeling wrong, and then I'd be hit with another spell.

Finally, Bruce took me see the doctor who was in charge on a Sunday at the Dallas Medical and Surgical Clinic right after I'd had a spell so bad that I thought I was going to pass out. The doctor, who Bruce knew from the time when he worked there, checked me thoroughly to find that there was nothing physically wrong with me, so he started asking me questions. Finally, I broke down and cried and told him about the family I'd lost and about thinking I was seeing my sister everywhere. Understanding what the source of the trouble was, he told me I needed to focus on the present. He made me understand that nothing was going to change the past and that my lost family would not return. Instead, he pointed out that I had a husband who loved me very much and two beautiful, healthy little girls who needed their mother and that this was what was important in life. He also frightened me by telling me that if I continued to dwell in the past instead of the present, I would end up in Terrell. Even as a foreigner to the country, I knew that Terrell was the city where the insane asylum was located. Then he sent me out and called Bruce back in, telling him that the worst thing he could do was to baby me as he'd been doing. He warned him that if I had another spell, he needed to just ignore me. Fortunately for him, he never had to face that moment. Bruce was so kind-hearted and loved me so much that he would do anything for me, but I know it would have been extremely hard for him to just ignore my suffering. The doctor's words were apparently all I needed. I never had another spell.

In 1949 my brother Robert had gotten a recording contract in the United States. When Brenda was about a year old, some friends of ours were planning on driving to California and invited me to go along with them to visit my brother, who was in Los Angeles at that time. Both Bruce and my friend Jo Abbott encouraged me to go, reminding me that I hadn't seen any of my family in such a long time and that this was a great opportunity. Jo said that she'd gladly keep the girls during the day, and Bruce said he would keep them at night and take them to his parents' house on the weekend. Neither of them could see any reason why I shouldn't go and enjoy myself. Robert was glad to have me come for a visit, too.

Barbara, Brenda, and me in 1950.

After I got to Robert's, I called often to make sure everything was OK at home. Each time Bruce assured me that everything was just fine and that I should just relax and have a good time. Although it was great to see

BRENDA HANCOCK

Robert again and to meet his friends, a couple of days before I was supposed to return, I decided to go home. I missed Bruce and the girls too much to enjoy myself, so I took the train in the afternoon and arrived in Dallas the next morning. From the train station, I took a taxi and went to Jo's apartment to pick up the girls.

Although Barbara was glad to see me, she and Eska Jean were playing on the floor and she'd been fine the whole time I was gone. Brenda, on the other hand, was in Eska Jean's bed just staring at the ceiling. Jo told me that's all she'd done the entire time I'd been gone, that she wouldn't eat or cry or do anything except look up at the ceiling. When I picked her up, she was burning up with fever. I don't think even living in Pleasant Heights was as bad as coming home to find my little girl so sick. Amazingly, I hadn't been home an hour when her fever broke, and she was fine. After that, she wouldn't let me out of her sight—I couldn't even go to the bathroom without her for quite a while. I was so angry with Bruce for not telling me Brenda was sick, but he said he didn't want to spoil my visit with my brother. I swore then that I would never leave my children again, regardless of the situation, and I never did.

One day when Bruce was delivering to Luby's Cafeteria across from Southern Methodist University, the supervisor of several Luby's Cafeterias, Mr. Leggatt, came up to Bruce and asked him if he'd like to come to work at the cafeteria to train for a management position. Since it was a lot more money, he decided to make the move. Financially, it was a great decision, but it meant that he no longer was home early in the evenings, and he also had to work weekends. Apparently, he did well because in less than a year he became the manager of Luby's across from SMU. Every Saturday night and Sunday early afternoon the girls and I would go to Luby's to eat with Bruce, giving him a little more time with the girls than the one day off he was given each week.

Shortly after that, Yvonne and I began taking classes at night to become American citizens. Her husband, L. C., would drive us once a week to a school in downtown Dallas where we studied the history and government of the United States as well as of Texas. Since Bruce had to work, once again Jo kept the girls while I was away. Before we could become citizens, we had to pass an extensive test as well as an interview session.

Fortunately, I had finished with the lessons before we decided to move into a house of our own in the suburbs. This time I had a nice two-bedroom, one-bath house in a brand-new housing addition complete with paved roads and all utilities. Not only did I have a bathroom complete with a bathtub, but I also got a washing machine and was able to do laundry at home. Shortly after we moved to the new house in Irving, I passed the test for citizenship. There at the swearing-in ceremony was my dear friend Yvonne, who had also passed, along with Bruce and our two girls. After the ceremony was over and I was officially an American, we all went to Luby's to have dinner and celebrate. Although I'd always thought of myself as being French, until that day when I finally became an American, I had been a person without a nationality. Now my life was truly focused on the present and the future with my American husband, American children, and American citizenship for myself.

Yvonne and me, new American citizens.　　Bruce, Brenda, me, and Barbara in 1955.

CHAPTER 21

Full Circle

Several really nice things happened after we moved to Irving. Perhaps the most long-lasting were the friendships Bruce and I made with the other new couples who moved into the neighborhood about the same time we did. A couple named Sam and Darcus Littrell and their little boy Rudy, who was about a year younger than Brenda, were moving in next door on the same day we moved in and introduced themselves during breaks between carrying things into their house. Their second child was due in October, just a few months after they moved in. Two doors down on the other side Becky and Harvey Hugman, who were expecting their first child in November, moved in two days later. Spending most holidays and many weekends together, the six of us formed a bond that lasted even after we had outgrown the little houses on Hawthorne Street. Our children grew up feeling like they were all brothers and sisters to one another. What seemed to work out best was that Sam and Darcus's second child was a little girl they named Kandy, while Becky and Harvey had two sons, Kerry and Bobby, making the group of children an even division between the boys and the girls. Not only did I still have my

Left side of table: Becky Hugman, Bruce, Sam Littrell, Kandy Littrell. *Right side of table:* Bobby Hugman, Harvey Hugman, Rudy Littrell, Darcus Littrell, and me at the back.

earlier friends, Jean, Jo, Yvonne, and Hélène that I still remained close to, but now I also had Darcus and Becky.

A big surprise happened one afternoon about a year after we moved into the house on Hawthorne Street. Bruce came in from the backyard and said that he could swear he saw Don and Jean's dog in the backyard behind ours. Even though I'd kept in touch with Jean, she hadn't said anything about moving. Sure enough, when we went back out into the yard, there were Don and Jean coming out of the house. Boy, was it ever great to have my first real friend living right in my backyard!

Since I had come to America, I had learned many new things, had many new experiences. Once Barbara started school, another new experience became necessary. One day when she stepped off the bus to come home, I saw that her coat had a big blob on it. When I asked her what had happened, she explained that the bus driver was chewing tobacco and when he spit, it landed on her coat. That would never do! I told Bruce I needed to learn to drive right away. The next morning we took Barbara to school and went to get a car for me. Within a week, I had learned how to drive and had my license. Never again did my children ride a bus to go to school. I was becoming a true American.

Another nice thing was that now that we had a home of our own, some of my family began to come visit. The first to arrive from France was my cousin, Robert, the grandson of my father's sister. While visiting some distant relatives in Ohio, he made it a point to come by and see me. During the several days of his visit, I managed to catch up on the family and he got to know my little girls and could pass along news of us to the family when he got back home. Next came my sister Aimée, who visited in 1953. She had come to New York to see our brother in "New Faces of 1952" and came on down to Texas to visit with me as well. Even though the visit wasn't long, it was really good to have her there. The one thing that these visits from family showed us was that the house was just a wee bit too small for company. Since Bruce had gotten a promotion and was making really good money as a manager, we decided to look for a larger house.

Not far away from where we lived a brand-new housing addition was being built just south of Highway 183. The houses there were brick with three bedrooms and two baths. Now, the girls could each have their own bedroom and share a bath separate from ours. In addition, the elementary school was relatively new. Barbara had been in the oldest school in the district, and its gloomy atmosphere contributed to her dislike of school. Hopefully, the bright new school would give both girls a better experience than Barbara's first year had been. On nice days, the school was close enough that the girls could walk home from school. When company came, the girls shared a room, making room for guests in the other bedroom. Shortly after we moved, Darcus and Sam moved to Betsy Lane as well, just four houses

From left: Brenda, Bruce, Barbara, and Robert in New York in 1954.

Bruce and me in New York in 1954.

down the street from us, and Becky and Harvey bought a house just on the other side of Highway 183, so we still managed to maintain those friendships.

Perhaps the most decisive moment in my "recovery" came just a few years after we moved to the house on Betsy Lane. One afternoon around two o'clock when the girls were at school and Bruce was at work, I answered a knock at the door. There stood a tall young man asking me in English if Bruce Holland happened to be home. When I explained that he was at work, he said, "I'm Emile Lebouluec." I never would have recognized Claudine and Louisette's younger brother since he'd been eleven years old the last time I saw him. Immediately, I told him to come on in. He responded that he couldn't come in because his wife was in the car. When I said that she should come in, too, he answered that she couldn't because she was German. His sisters had told him that I'd often said I would gladly watch a German die of thirst before I'd give him or her a drink of water. He knew that I'd lost many members of my family during the war to the Germans. Even his own father and brother refused to accept Gertie, his wife. He had just come by to say hello and let me know that he'd be working in Dallas as a chef at the Sheraton Hotel. Immediately, I told him to go get his wife and come in. His family had been so nice to me that I could not turn him away, even if he'd fallen in love with and married a German while he was serving in the American army. Although Gertie was a very nice, quiet young lady, I couldn't help but wonder if some of her family hadn't been responsible for the death of some of my family. Despite these thoughts, I opened my heart to this young woman. Milo, as I'd called him when he was a little boy, and Gertie stayed with us for several days while we helped them to find an apartment. When they had their first son, they all came back to our house from the hospital, and I helped her as my mother-in-law had helped me. Because of Gertie, I learned that I didn't need to continue to hate all Germans. It became very important to me to let my children know that each person needs to be judged on his or her own merits and that it is very wrong to hate any one group of people, regardless of the circumstances. Thanks to the Lebouluec family, first through their involvement with my meeting Bruce and then through my getting to know Gertie, my life had changed from focusing on loss and hatred to realizing the value of love and its healing powers.

Epilogue

Bruce and Nicole Holland lived in Texas for almost fifty-one years. After working for Luby's for nine years, Bruce took a job with Nationwide Food Service, which later became Canteen Corporation, as the supervisor of several cafeterias located in factories in the Dallas area as well as Texarkana. This enabled him to be home nights and weekends again, never too tired after a day's work to dance with the girls or sweep his beloved Nicky into his arms. In 1968 they moved to Daingerfield, Texas, where they owned and operated the Hill House Café for many years. Both girls married and each had two daughters. After her divorce, Brenda

From left: Bruce, Erbie, Dee Herbert, and Geneva in 1970s.

From left: Barbara, Bruce, Nicole, and Brenda in 1988.

married again and gained another daughter and a son. Barbara has two granddaughters and a grandson, while Brenda has three granddaughters and a grandson.

Nicole fought another battle beginning in 1980 when she was diagnosed with polymiositis, a muscle disease that almost made her an invalid. After a year-long battle, during which Bruce unfailingly took care of her and always let her know how much he loved her, Nicole won that battle, too, as the dis-

Bruce and me at our fiftieth wedding anniversary party.

ease went into remission. Seeing them dance together again was a miracle that brought tears to their daughters' eyes.

In 1997 Nicole and Bruce moved to Fayetteville, Arkansas, to be near both their daughters, who had relocated there. In 1999 just a few days after their fifty-third anniversary, Bruce died from a heart attack. Nicole currently keeps busy playing bridge and Mah Jong and visiting with friends in several clubs. In addition she talks with her brother Robert, who lives in California, and her sister Madeleine, at least once each week and occasionally the three of them get together in California for a visit.

Her lifelong friend Suzanne not only came to be with Nicky after Bruce's death, but

From left: Don and Jean Boldin with Sam and Darcus Littrell.

they also write and call each other frequently. As for Darcus and Sam, Becky and Harvey, and Don and Jean, and Bruce's family, Nicky sees them when she gets back to Texas and visits on the phone from time to time. She will never forget their acceptance, their help, and most important, the love they so willingly gave to her, especially knowing how many other French

From left: Bruce with Harvey and Becky Hugman, all at our fiftieth wedding anniversary party.

war brides came to America only to find families who never accepted them, never welcomed them as a new daughter.

In Paris, the apartment building on Rue des Deux Ponts that was first Nicole's family home, then her sister Madeleine's with her husband, Jean, and their two daughters and finally the home of her older sister Aimée and her husband, Gaston, has been renovated and become quite the stylish neighborhood. In 2007 a plaque was permanently attached to the front of the building to commemorate those who had lived there, been deported to concentration camps, and were exterminated in the death camps. The "M. Mme. Widerman et 1 enfant" in the right column are Nicole's parents and her sister Hélène.

The plaque reads "To the

Madeleine, Robert, and me at Robert's seventy-fifth birthday party in Los Angeles.

Suzanne and me in 2000.

memory of the inhabitants of the building at 10-12 Rue des Deux-Ponts (Street of the Two Bridges), deported from 1942 to 1944 because they were born Jewish, innocent victims of the barbarous Nazis with the complicity of the Vichy government." The plaque then lists those who died in concentration camps and concludes with "They were exterminated in the death camps. Never forget them. April 29, 2007."

Milo and Gertie Lebouluec, Louisette, me, and Claudine at my eightieth birthday party.

BRENDA HANCOCK

A LA MÉMOIRE DES HABITANTS DE L'IMMEUBLE 10-12 RUE DES DEUX-PONTS, DÉPORTÉS DE 1942 A 1944 PARCE CE QU'ILS ÉTAIENT NÉS JUIFS, VICTIMES INNOCENTES DE LA BARBARIE NAZIE AVEC LA COMPLICITÉ ACTIVE DU GOUVERNEMENT DE VICHY.

M. Mme ADONER et 5 enfants
Mme AROUS et 3 enfants
Les 3 jeunes BENDER
M. Mme CELEMENSKI et 2 enfants
M. CUKIERMAN (ZARKA)
M. Mme EINHORN et 2 enfants
M. Mme FEIGENOFF et 4 enfants
M. Mme FEINSTEIN et 2 enfants
Les 2 frères GALOWSKI
Frère et soeur GOLSTEIN
M. Mme GRUNFELD et 3 enfants
M. Mme HELWASER et 1 enfant
M. Mme KELLER et 2 enfants
M. Mme KLEIN et 3 enfants
Le jeune Henri KIONKOWSKI
M. Mme NOSSENSCHOUK

M. Mme ROZEMBERG et 2 enfants
M. ROZENZWEIG et 2 enfants
Mme SCHUSTER
M. Mme SCHWIMER et 2 enfants
M. Mme SMILIANSKI et 4 enfants
Mme STERNZUS et 2 enfants
M. Mme TARNEGUL
M. Mme WELGER et 3 enfants
M. Mme WIDERMAN et 1 enfant
M. WIDERMAN (WODZEK)
Mme Veuve WIOREK et 6 enfants
M. Mme WNOUK
M. Mme ZELICHEWSKI et 2 enfants
Mme ZYLBERBERG et 4 enfants
Mme ZYLBERBERG et 1 enfant
M. Mme KORENBLUT et 1 enfant

ILS FURENT EXTERMINÉS DANS LES CAMPS DE LA MORT.

LES OUBLIONS JAMAIS

Le 29 avril 2007

About the Author

Brenda Hancock , the younger daughter of Nicole Holland, grew up in Irving, Texas and graduated from East Texas State University (now Texas A & M at Commerce). A retired teacher, Brenda taught various levels of French, English, and math for 38 years in Texas, Missouri and Arkansas as well as with the Department of Defense Dependents Schools in Korea and Germany. She currently lives in Fayetteville, AR with her husband and their two spoiled rotten little dogs.